Timeless Secrets
Of A Warrior

By Mike Agugliaro

With contributions from some of history's great thinkers:

Russell H. Conwell, P. T. Barnum,
Orison Swett Marden, and James Allen

ISBN-13: 978-1530827855
ISBN-10: 153082785X

CONTENTS

ACTION STEPS: HOW TO GET THE MOST OUT OF THIS BOOK

You're reading this book because you want to grow your service business. But reading is only part of the process. I want you to be inspired and fully engaged throughout the process of business growth so I've listed several steps for you below. Think of it as an entry-level curriculum to grow your service business. Be sure to complete every step because they all work together.

1. **Read this book**. Actively read this book with a pen and highlighter in hand and a pad of paper and sticky notes nearby. Underline key points; add a star or exclamation point in the margin when you want something to stand out to you. On the pad of paper, make a list of the actions you'll take.

2. **Complete the action steps**. Throughout this book I've included sections called "Take Action!" Watch for these and when you get to them, complete each action step. Do them immediately.

3. **Bookmark CEOWARRIOR.com**: you'll find a wealth of resources to help you, including a blog, my upcoming events, and videos.

4. **Sign up for the newsletter at CEOWARRIOR.com**: this is a must-read newsletter that arrives in your email inbox weekly and you can sign up for it on the website above.

5. **Connect with me on social media:** Visit CEOWARRIOR.com to find all the social media channels we can connect on.

6. **Watch for my next Warrior Fast Track Academy**: Warrior Fast Track Academy is a 4-day event to help service business owners achieve real change and real success in their business. Make it a priority it attend! Learn more at WarriorFastTrackAcademy.com.

INTRODUCTION

Here's The Most Important Definition You Need To Know

This book is called *Timeless Secrets Of A Warrior*. When you saw the title, you might have wondered who the Warrior was and what that had to do with you. After all, you're not carrying a sword into battle.

So before we get into the book, and the Warrior secrets contained within, let's start by defining what a Warrior is… and why it should be of **massive importance to you, your life, your family, your wealth, your business, and your future.**

Imagine that you lived in ancient times. Life was simple but harsh: you survived through the simple acts of hunting and gathering… or you didn't survive. But it wasn't just the basic needs of food and water that determined your life; there were other forces that threatened your life as well. Opposing villages could swoop in and conquer (and often did); even wild animals made you keep a wary eye open at all times.

But among your small, ancient village was a group of people who were ready, willing, and able to step up and do whatever was necessary to protect everyone.

These were the **Warriors**. When called upon, the Warriors would arm themselves with sword, spear, and shield, they'd put on their helmet and armor, and they'd march toward the danger. They'd step up to the challenge – whatever the challenge happened to be.

Today, of course, the same heroes are embodied in our emergency services and military who similarly suit up and stand in harm's way to protect us.

Whether we're talking about modern Warriors or ancient Warriors, there are certain components that remain the same: **Warriors are bold and fearless action-takers who charge into the fray, leading others to follow them, and willingly spill blood for whatever cause they're fighting for.**

And that's the point I want to highlight: the Warrior mindset isn't reserved just for ancient or modern *soldiers* but for **anyone and everyone who wants to achieve something in their lives.**

What does it take for you to achieve success in business? It doesn't take just a small amount of action; rather, **it takes a Warrior's level of energy and drive**. What does it take for you to achieve success in life? Again, it doesn't take just a small amount of action; rather, it takes a Warrior's level of energy and drive.

Put yourself in the shoes of those ancient Warriors who stood across the battlefield from their foe…

Each Warrior is lined up, with spear or knife in one hand and their shield in the other. In between you and your enemy is an empty field that you know, in just a few short minutes, will be littered with the slain bodies of your brothers.

You stand on the front lines, perhaps shaking slightly from fear and anticipation. But in spite of that, everything is extra clear: you see the eyes of your enemy, you hear even their whispers, you think you can feel their heartbeats.

You know that very shortly you'll be using your weapons to draw blood and it's highly likely that your own blood will spill. You watch as others cowardly run away. But you stand your ground.

A battle cry is given and instantly your entire group launches from standing to charging. It takes every ounce of energy and courage to race across the uneven field, shouting as you go.

In an instant, you go from 100 yards away to 50 yards, 25 yards, 10 yards and closing fast. Above your own battlecry, you hear the clashing of weapons as the front lines meet.

... History is filled with thousands upon thousands of scenes just like that – some of them have been recorded for us by historians but many accounts have been lost to the ages.

Chances are, if you lived 2000 years ago or more, you probably would have lived through more than a few of those exact situations.

The Warrior Mind

Imagine what you would need inside of you to achieve victory in a situation like that. What qualities and personal characteristics would have allowed you to stand victorious at the end of such an event? Probably qualities like focus, courage, and perseverance, just to name a few.

Today, our modern world has insulated us from those qualities: we aren't often called up to become *military* Warriors anymore. As a society, we invest heavily into our own comfort – from our houses to our cars to our clothes – everything we buy has a layer of comfort and convenience built in. We spend so much time and energy helping children feel good about themselves, no matter what their level of achievement. We observe battle – we watch fictional conflicts on a big screen TV from the comfort of our living rooms while we drink carbonated beverages and eat popcorn. But we certainly don't live it.

The bottom line: **we've become a world focused on feel good immediacy rather than being willing to fight for the things we believe in.** Don't get me wrong: it's nice to have modern comforts and conveniences but those same conveniences have softened us. The **Warrior within us is asleep because someone else does the Warrior work** while we enjoy the comforts.

But what people don't realize is this: if you want something in life, you're going to have to **awaken that sleeping Warrior** because **it's going to take a Warrior's level of focus and courage and perseverance to achieve anything you want in life.**

That same level of personal determination and willpower to charge toward a screaming, sword-wielding enemy is the same level of determination and willpower that you'll need to tap into in yourself if you want to achieve any level of success.

I Want To Take You On A Journey Toward Becoming A Warrior

You'll notice that I use this Warrior language a lot. It's intentional. I think most of us are living lives on autopilot, just defaulting to the patterns and routines that are comfortable. But Warriors don't settle for that. **Warriors strip away the non-essentials and crash through the noise and distractions of life with a blistering force of will and motivation that demolishes any roadblock.**

If you want to achieve anything in your life, you need to become a Warrior. **Success in life, in business, in relationships, in wealth – in anything, actually – it's ONLY possible when you become a Warrior.**

It's for that reason that I created CEO Warrior, a brand that serves business owners like you, not only to give you the strategies and tools to battle against mediocrity in your business but also to reignite in you the fierce passion and drive of an ancient Warrior to go out and achieve whatever you want.

I want to give you all the **tools and strategies** you need to grow your business, and I want to share the **mindsets** and the Warrior way that are foundational for effectively implementing the tools and strategies.

In this book I've shared with you an invaluable resource to prepare you for the journey toward becoming a Warrior. And to help me, I've pulled together the writings of four of the world's great thinkers, who are each Warriors in their own way.

Each of these works are over one hundred years old but it would be naïve to dismiss them because of their age. In fact, as a lifelong martial artist, I can tell you that studying the ancient ways is a very powerful way to establish a foundation of knowledge and skills. The old ways aren't "old school," they were created by pioneers who established the path that we now walk on.

So, while many struggling service business owners might be looking for something shiny and new, I'm having you turn around and look back into history.

As Anthony Robbins says, "success leaves clues." Warriors study successful people who have gone before in order to pick up on the clues that they've left behind.

As you read these works, you'll probably become distracted (and perhaps even occasionally annoyed) at their writing; as I mentioned, each of these four works are over 100 years old.

But you need to remember this: they were all written in a certain cultural context that is different from today: the language they use, as well as the examples and stories they use, were relevant to their contemporary audiences. **(The truths in their writings is still relevant to us today**... But only if we make the one extra step of looking beyond the old school language).

As an example, you're going to read a lot about the Bible and about God in these. In fact, one of the writings is from a Christian minister. But the truths you read here apply to you whether or not you believe in any kind of higher power – you just need to remember that these works were written in a culture and age where the Bible was a familiar book and everyone went to church.

Today it's different (and someone reading a modern book 100 years from now will wonder why today's writers talk about Facebook so often – it's the same concept as us reading about religious references from a century ago).

People who are on their way to becoming Warriors will find tremendous value in this information and will eagerly read each lesson with the understanding that the truths in here are timeless. (Likewise, I don't dismiss any of my martial arts education just because I live thousands of years later in a totally different culture than those who developed the initial moves and strategies; I willingly step up and study it more deeply because it has survived for so long. THAT is how you should approach this book.)

Moreover, these writers were writing strategies that they knew worked, yet some of these secrets have become lost over time. That's why it's so important to read information that some people believe is "old" or even "outdated" – because smart Warriors know that they'll uncover powerful ideas that can get lost over time.

I've done all the work of "mining" this information – now it's your turn to read it.

Here's How To Read This Book

If you agree that there is value in the ideas and strategies forged by pioneering minds, and if you are willing to learn in order to reignite the passion and courage of the Warrior within you, then let me help you.

We stand on the banks of a river looking at the thought-leading pioneers. They stand on the other side. Let me show you how to build a bridge.

This book contains the works of four writers.

When you turn to a work in this book, I give you the title and then I introduce the writer, their work and why I've specially chosen this writing to be included as a lesson for you. I connect it to specific ideas related to owning a service business. Then I let this Warrior from history "speak" to you with their writings (and I have included my own "Warrior Wisdom" interspersed throughout the book to help connect their ideas to modern life).

With the exception of my own thoughts – Warrior Wisdom – I have provided these Warriors' works almost completely untouched. You're getting their full thought on a topic. Sometimes their language and even their spelling is old school. (Don't worry, it's not as hard to read as Shakespeare – it's still modern English but they use slightly older terminology). I could have gone through and revised or hired an editor to rewrite and modernize it all but I'd be doing you a disservice: To be frank, I want you to work for the lessons because, as I've learned in martial arts, **the lessons that you work for are the ones that stick.**

So here's what I want you to do: get a pencil and a highlighter and start reading. Make notes as you go. Highlight the key ideas. In the margins, make notes on how it applies to you. I want you to extract specific actions that you can take (including ways to change your thinking, new habits to adopt, old habits to break). Make a list. **Every single time I read these works I end up with a HUGE list of actions to start doing, actions to stop doing, and actions to continue doing – and I believe you will too.**

At the back of each of these writings I have included a worksheet that you can write on. If you run out of space, use a blank piece of paper.

Your book will say a lot about a person: Those with pristine books that have barely been opened (and may have a layer of dust on them) versus those who have books that look beat up because they are filled with notes and highlights from multiple readings. Guess which person gets the most value from the book? And not surprisingly, guess which person grows the most.

Now get your pen and highlighter, turn the page, and dive into some of the lessons from history's great thinkers. **There's a lot to learn and if you want to be a Warrior then you'll step up and devour their teachings.**

ACRES OF DIAMONDS

Introduction By Mike Agugliaro

The first reading comes from a man named Russell H. Conwell. He lived from 1843 to 1925. Conwell served in the Union Army in the Civil War and later became a Baptist Minister and founder of Temple University in Philadelphia.

In 1913, Conwell gave a speech to a reunion of his military comrades. The speech was well received and he went on to give the same speech around the world more than 6,000 times. That speech is called "Acres Of Diamonds." I'm including the transcript of his speech here.

If you quickly scan the speech, you may become distracted by the dated words and storytelling, and by many references to his faith. And if that's all you get from this speech, you will have missed the point. There's a reason he gave this speech more than 6,000 times – **it remains an inspiring speech about discovering opportunity and achieving greatness.** Its lessons are as true today as they were a century ago when he gave the speech.

Here's what I want you to pay attention to:

- Notice what Conwell describes as "opportunity" and pay attention to where he says this opportunity exists. As you read, make the connection to your own life and business and examine closely where your opportunities are.
- Also, notice how he references greatness, and who he says can achieve it. In particular, pay attention to when and how someone can be great.

I may not use the same words as Conwell but I frequently talk about the same concepts – that **opportunity and greatness are within your reach** (you just may not realize it). I also drill down and focus in on where opportunity exists for you in your own service business, and how greatness can be achieved in your life.

Conwell may sound old fashioned but his popular speech is as true today as it was when he gave it. A true modern-day Warrior will listen carefully to every word Conwell gives and consider how it impacts him today.

Now let's dive in to Conwell's timeless secrets...

Acres Of Diamonds By Russell Conwell

When going down the Tigris and Euphrates rivers many years ago with a party of English travelers I found myself under the direction of an old Arab guide whom we hired up at Bagdad, and I have often thought how that guide resembled our barbers in certain mental characteristics. He thought that it was not only his duty to guide us down those rivers, and do what he was paid for doing, but also to entertain us with stories curious and weird, ancient and modern, strange and familiar. Many of them I have forgotten, and I am glad I have, but there is one I shall never forget.

The old guide was leading my camel by its halter along the banks of those ancient rivers, and he told me story after story until I grew weary of his story-telling and ceased to listen. I have never been irritated with that guide when he lost his temper as I ceased listening.

But I remember that he took off his Turkish cap and swung it in a circle to get my attention. I could see it through the corner of my eye, but I determined not to look straight at him for fear he would tell another story. But although I am not a woman, I did finally look, and as soon as I did he went right into another story.

Said he, "I will tell you a story now which I reserve for my particular friends." When he emphasized the words "particular friends," I listened, and I have ever been glad I did. I really feel devoutly thankful, that there are 1,674 young men who have been carried through college by this lecture who are also glad that I did listen.

 **Warrior Wisdom**: there is so much power in listening – even to those we might not immediately realize have lessons to teach us.

-Mike Agugliaro

The old guide told me that there once lived not far from the River Indus an ancient Persian by the name of Ali Hafed. He said that Ali Hafed owned a very large farm, that he had orchards, grain-fields, and gardens; that he had money at interest, and was a wealthy and contented man.

14

He was contented because he was wealthy, and wealthy because he was contented. One day there visited that old Persian farmer one of these ancient Buddhist priests, one of the wise men of the East. He sat down by the fire and told the old farmer how this world of ours was made. He said that this world was once a mere bank of fog, and that the Almighty thrust His finger into this bank of fog, and began slowly to move His finger around, increasing the speed until at last He whirled this bank of fog into a solid ball of fire. Then it went rolling through the universe, burning its way through other banks of fog, and condensed the moisture without, until it fell in floods of rain upon its hot surface, and cooled the outward crust.

Then the internal fires bursting outward through the crust threw up the mountains and hills, the valleys, the plains and prairies of this wonderful world of ours. If this internal molten mass came bursting out and cooled very quickly it became granite; less quickly copper, less quickly silver, less quickly gold, and, after gold, diamonds were made.

Said the old priest, "A diamond is a congealed drop of sunlight." Now that is literally scientifically true, that a diamond is an actual deposit of carbon from the sun. The old priest told Ali Hafed that if he had one diamond the size of his thumb he could purchase the county, and if he had a mine of diamonds he could place his children upon thrones through the influence of their great wealth.

Ali Hafed heard all about diamonds, how much they were worth, and went to his bed that night a poor man. He had not lost anything, but he was poor because he was discontented, and discontented because he feared he was poor. He said, "I want a mine of diamonds," and he lay awake all night.

Early in the morning he sought out the priest. I know by experience that a priest is very cross when awakened early in the morning, and when he shook that old priest out of his dreams, Ali Hafed said to him:

"Will you tell me where I can find diamonds?"

"Diamonds! What do you want with diamonds?"

"Why, I wish to be immensely rich."

"Well, then, go along and find them. That is all you have to do; go and find them, and then you have them."

"But I don't know where to go."

"Well, if you will find a river that runs through white sands, between high mountains, in those white sands you will always find diamonds."

"I don't believe there is any such river."

"Oh yes, there are plenty of them. All you have to do is to go and find them, and then you have them."

Said Ali Hafed, "I will go."

So he sold his farm, collected his money, left his family in charge of a neighbor, and away he went in search of diamonds. He began his search, very properly to my mind, at the Mountains of the Moon. Afterward he came around into Palestine, then wandered on into Europe, and at last when his money was all spent and he was in rags, wretchedness, and poverty, he stood on the shore of that bay at Barcelona, in Spain, when a great tidal wave came rolling in between the pillars of Hercules, and the poor, afflicted, suffering, dying man could not resist the awful temptation to cast himself into that incoming tide, and he sank beneath its foaming crest, never to rise in this life again.

When that old guide had told me that awfully sad story he stopped the camel I was riding on and went back to fix the baggage that was coming off another camel, and I had an opportunity to muse over his story while he was gone. I remember saying to myself, "Why did he reserve that story for his 'particular friends'?" There seemed to be no beginning, no middle, no end, nothing to it. That was the first story I had ever heard told in my life, and would be the first one I ever read, in which the hero was killed in the first chapter. I had but one chapter of that story, and the hero was dead.

When the guide came back and took up the halter of my camel, he went right ahead with the story, into the second chapter, just as though there had been no break...

The man who purchased Ali Hafed's farm one day led his camel into the garden to drink, and as that camel put its nose into the shallow water of that garden brook, Ali Hafed's successor noticed a curious flash of light from the white sands of the stream. He pulled out a black stone having an eye of light reflecting all the hues of the rainbow. He took the pebble into the house and put it on the mantel which covers the central fires, and forgot all about it.

A few days later this same old priest came in to visit Ali Hafed's successor, and the moment he opened that drawing-room door he saw that flash of light on the mantel, and he rushed up to it, and shouted: "Here is a diamond! Has Ali Hafed returned?"

"Oh no, Ali Hafed has not returned, and that is not a diamond. That is nothing but a stone we found right out here in our own garden."

"But," said the priest, "I tell you I know a diamond when I see it. I know positively that is a diamond."

Then together they rushed out into that old garden and stirred up the white sands with their fingers, and lo! there came up other more beautiful and valuable gems than the first.

"Thus," said the guide to me, and, friends, it is historically true, "was discovered the diamond-mine of Golconda, the most magnificent diamond-mine in all the history of mankind, excelling the Kimberly itself. The Kohinoor, and the Orloff of the crown jewels of England and Russia, the largest on earth, came from that mine."

When that old Arab guide told me the second chapter of his story, he then took off his Turkish cap and swung it around in the air again to get my attention to the moral. Those Arab guides have morals to their stories, although they are not always moral. As he swung his hat, he said to me, "Had Ali Hafed remained at home and dug in his own cellar, or underneath his own wheat-fields, or in his own garden, instead of wretchedness, starvation, and death by suicide in a strange land, he would have had 'acres of diamonds.' For every acre of that old farm, yes, every shovelful, afterward revealed gems which since have decorated the crowns of monarchs."

 **Warrior Wisdom**: in every business, in every market, there are "acres of diamonds." I see them all the time (even in the markets of those who claim that they're all "mined out"). In nearly every service business, the overlooked acres of diamonds include: people, growth, profit, added services, and so much more.

-Mike Agugliaro

When he had added the moral to his story I saw why he reserved it for "his particular friends." But I did not tell him I could see it. It was that mean old Arab's way of going around a thing like a lawyer, to say indirectly what he did not dare say directly, that "in his private opinion there was a certain young man then traveling down the Tigris River that might better be at home in America." I did not tell him I could see that, but I told him his story reminded me of one, and I told it to him quick, and I think I will tell it to you.

I told him of a man out in California in 1847 who owned a ranch. He heard they had discovered gold in southern California, and so with a passion for gold he sold his ranch to Colonel Sutter, and away he went, never to come back. Colonel Sutter put a mill upon a stream that ran through that ranch, and one day his little girl brought some wet sand from the raceway into their home and sifted it through her fingers before the fire, and in that falling sand a visitor saw the first shining scales of real gold that were ever discovered in California. The man who had owned that ranch wanted gold, and he could have secured it for the mere taking. Indeed, thirty-eight millions of dollars has been taken out of a very few acres since then. About eight years ago I delivered this lecture in a city that stands on that farm, and they told me that a one-third owner for years and years had been getting one hundred and twenty dollars in gold every fifteen minutes, sleeping or waking, without taxation.

You and I would enjoy an income like that—if we didn't have to pay an income tax.

But a better illustration really than that occurred here in our own Pennsylvania. If there is anything I enjoy above another on the platform, it is to get one of these German audiences in Pennsylvania before me, and fire that at them, and I enjoy it to-night. There was a man living in Pennsylvania, not unlike some Pennsylvanians you have seen, who owned a farm, and he did with that farm just what I should do with a farm if I owned one in Pennsylvania--he sold it. But before he sold it he decided to secure employment collecting coal-oil for his cousin, who was in the business in Canada, where they first discovered oil on this continent. They dipped it from the running streams at that early time. So this Pennsylvania farmer wrote to his cousin asking for employment. You see, friends, this farmer was not altogether a foolish man. No, he was not. He did not leave his farm until he had something else to do. Of all the simpletons the stars shine on I don't know of a worse one than the man who leaves one job before he has gotten another.

That has especial reference to my profession, and has no reference whatever to a man seeking a divorce. When he wrote to his cousin for employment, his cousin replied, "I cannot engage you because you know nothing about the oil business."

Well, then the old farmer said, "I will know," and with most commendable zeal (characteristic of the students of Temple University) he set himself at the study of the whole subject. He began away back at the second day of God's creation when this world was covered thick and deep with that rich vegetation which since has turned to the primitive beds of coal. He studied the subject until he found that the drainings really of those rich beds of coal furnished the coal-oil that was worth pumping, and then he found how it came up with the living springs. He studied until he knew what it looked like, smelled like, tasted like, and how to refine it.

Now said he in his letter to his cousin, "I understand the oil business."

His cousin answered, "All right, come on."

So he sold his farm, according to the county record, for $833 (even money, "no cents"). He had scarcely gone from that place before the man who purchased the spot went out to arrange for the watering of the cattle. He found the previous owner had gone out years before and put a plank across the brook back of the barn, edgewise into the surface of the water just a few inches. The purpose of that plank at that sharp angle across the brook was to throw over to the other bank a dreadful-looking scum through which the cattle would not put their noses. But with that plank there to throw it all over to one side, the cattle would drink below, and thus that man who had gone to Canada had been himself damming back for twenty-three years a flood of

18

coal-oil which the state geologists of Pennsylvania declared to us ten years later was even then worth a hundred millions of dollars to our state, and four years ago our geologist declared the discovery to be worth to our state a thousand millions of dollars. The man who owned that territory on which the city of Titusville now stands, and those Pleasantville valleys, had studied the subject from the second day of God's creation clear down to the present time. He studied it until he knew all about it, and yet he is said to have sold the whole of it for $833, and again I say, "no sense."

Warrior Wisdom: sometimes our own knowledge, assumptions, and limiting beliefs get in our way and keep us from seeing the true riches that exist right before our eyes.

-Mike Agugliaro

But I need another illustration. I found it in Massachusetts, and I am sorry I did because that is the state I came from. This young man in Massachusetts furnishes just another phase of my thought. He went to Yale College and studied mines and mining, and became such an adept as a mining engineer that he was employed by the authorities of the university to train students who were behind their classes. During his senior year he earned $15 a week for doing that work. When he graduated they raised his pay from $15 to $45 a week, and offered him a professorship, and as soon as they did he went right home to his mother.

If they had raised that boy's pay from $15 to $15.60 he would have stayed and been proud of the place, but when they put it up to $45 at one leap, he said, "Mother, I won't work for $45 a week. The idea of a man with a brain like mine working for $45 a week! Let's go out in California and stake out gold-mines and silver-mines, and be immensely rich."

Said his mother, "Now, Charlie, it is just as well to be happy as it is to be rich."

"Yes," said Charlie, "but it is just as well to be rich and happy, too." And they were both right about it. As he was an only son and she a widow, of course he had his way. They always do.

They sold out in Massachusetts, and instead of going to California they went to Wisconsin, where he went into the employ of the Superior Copper Mining Company at $15 a week again, but with the proviso in his contract that he should have an interest in any mines he should discover for the company. I don't believe he ever discovered a mine, and if I am looking in the face of any stockholder of that copper company you wish he had discovered something

19

or other. I have friends who are not here because they could not afford a ticket, who did have stock in that company at the time this young man was employed there. This young man went out there, and I have not heard a word from him. I don't know what became of him, and I don't know whether he found any mines or not, but I don't believe he ever did.

But I do know the other end of the line. He had scarcely gotten out of the old homestead before the succeeding owner went out to dig potatoes. The potatoes were already growing in the ground when he bought the farm, and as the old farmer was bringing in a basket of potatoes it hugged very tight between the ends of the stone fence. You know in Massachusetts our farms are nearly all stone wall. There you are obliged to be very economical of front gateways in order to have some place to put the stone. When that basket hugged so tight he set it down on the ground, and then dragged on one side, and pulled on the other side, and as he was dragging that basket through this farmer noticed in the upper and outer corner of that stone wall, right next the gate, a block of native silver eight inches square. That professor of mines, mining, and mineralogy who knew so much about the subject that he would not work for $45 a week, when he sold that homestead in Massachusetts sat right on that silver to make the bargain. He was born on that homestead, was brought up there, and had gone back and forth rubbing the stone with his sleeve until it reflected his countenance, and seemed to say, "Here is a hundred thousand dollars right down here just for the taking." But he would not take it. It was in a home in Newburyport, Massachusetts, and there was no silver there, all away off--well, I don't know where, and he did not, but somewhere else, and he was a professor of mineralogy.

Warrior Wisdom: there is value to head knowledge but only if it serves you. Always learn, but be the master of your own knowledge; don't let it master you.

-Mike Agugliaro

My friends, that mistake is very universally made, and why should we even smile at him. I often wonder what has become of him. I do not know at all, but I will tell you what I "guess" as a Yankee. I guess that he sits out there by his fireside to-night with his friends gathered around him, and he is saying to them something like this: "Do you know that man Conwell who lives in Philadelphia?"

"Oh yes, I have heard of him."

"Do you know that man Jones that lives in Philadelphia?" "Yes, I have heard of him, too."

Then he begins to laugh, and shakes his sides and says to his friends, "Well, they have done just the same thing I did, precisely" – and that spoils the whole joke, for you and I have done the same thing he did, and while we sit here and laugh at him he has a better right to sit out there and laugh at us. I know I have made the same mistakes, but, of course, that does not make any difference, because we don't expect the same man to preach and practise, too.

As I come here to-night and look around this audience I am seeing again what through these fifty years I have continually seen-men that are making precisely that same mistake. I often wish I could see the younger people, and would that the Academy had been filled tonight with our high-school scholars and our grammar-school scholars, that I could have them to talk to. While I would have preferred such an audience as that, because they are most susceptible, as they have not grown up into their prejudices as we have, they have not gotten into any custom that they cannot break, they have not met with any failures as we have; and while I could perhaps do such an audience as that more good than I can do grown-up people, yet I will do the best I can with the material I have.

I say to you that you have "acres of diamonds" in Philadelphia right where you now live. "Oh," but you will say, "you cannot know much about your city if you think there are any 'acres of diamonds' here."

Warrior Wisdom: what are the acres of diamonds in your business and your market? Before you answer "none at all," consider the lessons that you've just read and spend some time giving serious thought to your answer.

-Mike Agugliaro

I was greatly interested in that account in the newspaper of the young man who found that diamond in North Carolina. It was one of the purest diamonds that has ever been discovered, and it has several predecessors near the same locality. I went to a distinguished professor in mineralogy and asked him where he thought those diamonds came from. The professor secured the map of the geologic formations of our continent, and traced it. He said it went either through the underlying carboniferous strata adapted for such production, westward through Ohio and the Mississippi, or in more probability came eastward through Virginia and up the shore of the Atlantic Ocean. It is a fact that the diamonds were there, for they have been discovered and sold; and that they were carried down there during the drift period, from some northern locality. Now who can say but some person going down with his drill in Philadelphia will find some trace of a diamond-mine yet down here?

Oh, friends! you cannot say that you are not over one of the greatest diamond-mines in the world, for such a diamond as that only comes from the most profitable mines that are found on earth.

But it serves simply to illustrate my thought, which I emphasize by saying if you do not have the actual diamond-mines literally you have all that they would be good for to you. Because now that the Queen of England has given the greatest compliment ever conferred upon American woman for her attire because she did not appear with any jewels at all at the late reception in England, it has almost done away with the use of diamonds anyhow. All you would care for would be the few you would wear if you wish to be modest, and the rest you would sell for money.

Now then, I say again that the opportunity to get rich, to attain unto great wealth, is here in Philadelphia now, within the reach of almost every man and woman who hears me speak to-night, and I mean just what I say. I have not come to this platform even under these circumstances to recite something to you. I have come to tell you what in God's sight I believe to be the truth, and if the years of life have been of any value to me in the attainment of common sense, I know I am right; that the men and women sitting here, who found it difficult perhaps to buy a ticket to this lecture or gathering to-night, have within their reach "acres of diamonds," opportunities to get largely wealthy. There never was a place on earth more adapted than the city of Philadelphia to-day, and never in the history of the world did a poor man without capital have such an opportunity to get rich quickly and honestly as he has now in our city.

Warrior Wisdom: read the above paragraph again, but instead of "Philadelphia", replace it with your own market. Read it slowly and feel the weight of the truth in those words.

-Mike Agugliaro

I say it is the truth, and I want you to accept it as such; for if you think I have come to simply recite something, then I would better not be here. I have no time to waste in any such talk, but to say the things I believe, and unless some of you get richer for what I am saying to-night my time is wasted.

I say that you ought to get rich, and it is your duty to get rich. How many of my pious brethren say to me, "Do you, a Christian minister, spend your time going up and down the country advising young people to get rich, to get money?" "Yes, of course I do." They say, "Isn't that awful! Why don't you preach the gospel instead of preaching about man's making money?" "Because to make money honestly is to preach the gospel."

That is the reason. The men who get rich may be the most honest men you find in the community.

"Oh," but says some young man here to-night, "I have been told all my life that if a person has money he is very dishonest and dishonorable and mean and contemptible." My friend, that is the reason why you have none, because you have that idea of people. The foundation of your faith is altogether false. Let me say here clearly, and say it briefly, though subject to discussion which I have not time for here, ninety-eight out of one hundred of the rich men of America are honest. That is why they are rich. That is why they are trusted with money. That is why they carry on great enterprises and find plenty of people to work with them. It is because they are honest men.

Warrior Wisdom: wealth and honesty are two separate things. Do not confuse the two. Always set a high ethical standard and pursue wealth – and enjoy the freedom your wealth brings.

-Mike Agugliaro

Says another young man, "I hear sometimes of men that get millions of dollars dishonestly." Yes, of course you do, and so do I. But they are so rare a thing in fact that the newspapers talk about them all the time as a matter of news until you get the idea that all the other rich men got rich dishonestly.

My friend, you take and drive me--if you furnish the auto--out into the suburbs of Philadelphia, and introduce me to the people who own their homes around this great city, those beautiful homes with gardens and flowers, those magnificent homes so lovely in their art, and I will introduce you to the very best people in character as well as in enterprise in our city, and you know I will. A man is not really a true man until he owns his own home, and they that own their homes are made more honorable and honest and pure, and true and economical and careful, by owning the home.

For a man to have money, even in large sums, is not an inconsistent thing. We preach against covetousness, and you know we do, in the pulpit, and oftentimes preach against it so long and use the terms about "filthy lucre" so extremely that Christians get the idea that when we stand in the pulpit we believe it is wicked for any man to have money--until the collection-basket goes around, and then we almost swear at the people because they don't give more money. Oh, the inconsistency of such doctrines as that!

Money is power, and you ought to be reasonably ambitious to have it. You ought because you can do more good with it than you could without it. Money printed your Bible, money builds your churches, money sends your missionaries, and money pays your preachers, and you would not have many of them, either, if you did not pay them. I am always willing that my church should raise my salary, because the church that pays the largest salary always raises it the easiest. You never knew an exception to it in your life. The man who gets the largest salary can do the most good with the power that is furnished to him. Of course he can if his spirit be right to use it for what it is given to him.

I say, then, you ought to have money. If you can honestly attain unto riches in Philadelphia, it is your Christian and godly duty to do so. It is an awful mistake of these pious people to think you must be awfully poor in order to be pious.

Some men say, "Don't you sympathize with the poor people?" Of course I do, or else I would not have been lecturing these years. I won't give in but what I sympathize with the poor, but the number of poor who are to be sympathized with is very small. To sympathize with a man whom God has punished for his sins, thus to help him when God would still continue a just punishment, is to do wrong, no doubt about it, and we do that more than we help those who are deserving. While we should sympathize with God's poor-- that is, those who cannot help themselves--let us remember there is not a poor person in the United States who was not made poor by his own shortcomings, or by the shortcomings of someone else. It is all wrong to be poor, anyhow. Let us give in to that argument and pass that to one side.

Warrior Wisdom: wealth allows us to help others – such as by providing them with jobs, or by supporting charities that help those who cannot help themselves.

-Mike Agugliaro

A gentleman gets up back there, and says, "Don't you think there are some things in this world that are better than money?" Of course I do, but I am talking about money now. Of course there are some things higher than money. Oh yes, I know by the grave that has left me standing alone that there are some things in this world that are higher and sweeter and purer than money. Well do I know there are some things higher and grander than gold. Love is the grandest thing on God's earth, but fortunate the lover who has plenty of money. Money is power, money is force, money will do good as well as harm. In the hands of good men and women it could accomplish, and it has accomplished, good.

Warrior Wisdom: money is a tool; it's innate. It is used for good or evil purposes. So if you are consciously or unconsciously avoiding money because you've come to believe that it's bad, that makes as little sense as avoiding a screwdriver or pliers because you think they are bad.

-Mike Agugliaro

I hate to leave that behind me. I heard a man get up in a prayer-meeting in our city and thank the Lord he was "one of God's poor." Well, I wonder what his wife thinks about that? She earns all the money that comes into that house, and he smokes a part of that on the veranda. I don't want to see any more of the Lord's poor of that kind, and I don't believe the Lord does. And yet there are some people who think in order to be pious you must be awfully poor and awfully dirty. That does not follow at all. While we sympathize with the poor, let us not teach a doctrine like that.

Yet the age is prejudiced against advising a Christian man (or, as a Jew would say, a godly man) from attaining unto wealth. The prejudice is so universal and the years are far enough back, I think, for me to safely mention that years ago up at Temple University there was a young man in our theological school who thought he was the only pious student in that department. He came into my office one evening and sat down by my desk, and said to me: "Mr. President, I think it is my duty sir, to come in and labor with you." "What has happened now?" Said he, "I heard you say at the Academy, at the Peirce School commencement, that you thought it was an honorable ambition for a young man to desire to have wealth, and that you thought it made him temperate, made him anxious to have a good name, and made him industrious. You spoke about man's ambition to have money helping to make him a good man. Sir, I have come to tell you the Holy Bible says that 'money is the root of all evil.'"

Warrior Wisdom: our limiting beliefs entered our minds from as far back as our childhood — whenever our parents or teachers taught us something they believed, or whenever they demonstrated with their lives a belief they held. But just because they taught it or believed it, doesn't make it true. Your challenge is to identify that limiting belief about money and address it.

-Mike Agugliaro

I told him I had never seen it in the Bible, and advised him to go out into the chapel and get the Bible, and show me the place. So out he went for the Bible, and soon he stalked into my office with the Bible open, with all the bigoted pride of the narrow sectarian, or of one who founds his Christianity on some misinterpretation of Scripture. He flung the Bible down on my desk, and fairly squealed into my ear: "There it is, Mr. President; you can read it for yourself." I said to him: "Well, young man, you will learn when you get a little older that you cannot trust another denomination to read the Bible for you. You belong to another denomination. You are taught in the theological school, however, that emphasis is exegesis. Now, will you take that Bible and read it yourself, and give the proper emphasis to it?"

He took the Bible, and proudly read, "'The love of money is the root of all evil.'"

Then he had it right, and when one does quote aright from that same old Book he quotes the absolute truth. I have lived through fifty years of the mightiest battle that old Book has ever fought, and I have lived to see its banners flying free; for never in the history of this world did the great minds of earth so universally agree that the Bible is true -- all true — as they do at this very hour.

So I say that when he quoted right, of course he quoted the absolute truth. "The love of money is the root of all evil." He who tries to attain unto it too quickly, or dishonestly, will fall into many snares, no doubt about that. The love of money. What is that? It is making an idol of money, and idolatry pure and simple everywhere is condemned by the Holy Scriptures and by man's common sense. The man that worships the dollar instead of thinking of the purposes for which it ought to be used, the man who idolizes simply money, the miser that hordes his money in the cellar, or hides it in his stocking, or refuses to invest it where it will do the world good, that man who hugs the dollar until the eagle squeals has in him the root of all evil.

Warrior Wisdom: don't miss the key lesson above – our beliefs about what we *think we know* shape how we act in the future. Will the things you know right now serve you in the future? Or do you need to change what you know?

-Mike Agugliaro

I think I will leave that behind me now and answer the question of nearly all of you who are asking, "Is there opportunity to get rich in Philadelphia?" Well, now, how simple a thing it is to see where it is, and the instant you see where it is it is yours. Some old gentleman gets up back there and says, "Mr. Conwell, have you lived in Philadelphia for thirty-one years and don't know that the time has gone by when you can make anything in this city?" "No, I don't think it is." "Yes, it is; I have tried it." "What business are you in?" "I kept a store here for twenty years, and never made over a thousand dollars in the whole twenty years."

"Well, then, you can measure the good you have been to this city by what this city has paid you, because a man can judge very well what he is worth by what he receives; that is, in what he is to the world at this time. If you have not made over a thousand dollars in twenty years in Philadelphia, it would have been better for Philadelphia if they had kicked you out of the city nineteen years and nine months ago. A man has no right to keep a store in Philadelphia twenty years and not make at least five hundred thousand dollars even though it be a corner grocery up-town." You say, "You cannot make five thousand dollars in a store now." Oh, my friends, if you will just take only four blocks around you, and find out what the people want and what you ought to supply and set them down with your pencil and figure up the profits you would make if you did supply them, you would very soon see it. There is wealth right within the sound of your voice.

Warrior Wisdom: *"there is wealth right within the sound of your voice"* – that is a powerful statement and I urge you to embed it into your brain.

-Mike Agugliaro

Someone says: "You don't know anything about business. A preacher never knows a thing about business." Well, then, I will have to prove that I am an expert. I don't like to do this, but I have to do it because my testimony will not be taken if I am not an expert. My father kept a country store, and if there is any place under the stars where a man gets all sorts of experience in every kind of mercantile transactions, it is in the country store. I am not proud of my experience, but sometimes when my father was away he would leave me in charge of the store, though fortunately for him that was not very often. But this did occur many times, friends: A man would come in the store, and say to me, "Do you keep jack knives?"

"No, we don't keep jack-knives," and I went off whistling a tune. What did I care about that man, anyhow?

Then another farmer would come in and say, "Do you keep jack knives?"

"No, we don't keep jack-knives." Then I went away and whistled another tune.

Then a third man came right in the same door and said, "Do you keep jack-knives?"

"No. Why is everyone around here asking for jack-knives? Do you suppose we are keeping this store to supply the whole neighborhood with jack-knives?"

Warrior Wisdom: what are people asking you for that you have been saying "no" to? Is there a skillset that is an untapped profit center for you?

-Mike Agugliaro

Do you carry on your store like that in Philadelphia? The difficulty was I had not then learned that the foundation of godliness and the foundation principle of success in business are both the same precisely. The man who says, "I cannot carry my religion into business" advertises himself either as being an imbecile in business, or on the road to bankruptcy, or a thief, one of the three, sure. He will fail within a very few years. He certainly will if he doesn't carry his religion into business. If I had been carrying on my father's store on a Christian plan, godly plan, I would have had a jack-knife for the third man when he called for it. Then I would have actually done him a kindness, and I would have received a reward myself, which it would have been my duty to take.

There are some over-pious Christian people who think if you take any profit on anything you sell that you are an unrighteous man. On the contrary, you would be a criminal to sell goods for less than they cost. You have no right to do that. You cannot trust a man with your money who cannot take care of his own. You cannot trust a man in your family that is not true to his own wife. You cannot trust a man in the world that does not begin with his own heart, his own character, and his own life. It would have been my duty to have furnished a jack-knife to the third man, or the second, and to have sold it to him and actually profited myself. I have no more right to sell goods without making a profit on them than I have to overcharge him dishonestly beyond what they are worth. But I should so sell each bill of goods that the person to whom I sell shall make as much as I make.

To live and let live is the principle of the gospel, and the principle of every-day common sense. Oh, young man, hear me; live as you go along. Do not wait until you have reached my years before you begin to enjoy anything of this life. If I had the millions back, or fifty cents of it, which I have tried to earn in these years, it would not do me anything like the good that it does me now in this almost sacred presence to-night. Oh, yes, I am paid over and over a hundredfold to-night for dividing as I have tried to do in some measure as I went along through the years. I ought not speak that way, it sounds egotistic, but I am old enough now to be excused for that. I should have helped my fellow-men, which I have tried to do, and everyone should try to do, and get the happiness of it. The man who goes home with the sense that he has stolen a dollar that day, that he has robbed a man of what was his honest due, is not going to sweet rest. He arises tired in the morning, and goes with an unclean conscience to his work the next day. He is not a successful man at all, although he may have laid up millions. But the man who has gone through life dividing always with his fellow-men, making and demanding his own rights and his own profits, and giving to every other man his rights and profits, lives every day, and not only that, but it is the royal road to great wealth. The history of the thousands of millionaires shows that to be the case.

The man over there who said he could not make anything in a store in Philadelphia has been carrying on his store on the wrong principle. Suppose I go into your store to-morrow morning and ask, "Do you know neighbor A, who lives one square away, at house No. 1240?"

"Oh yes, I have met him. He deals here at the corner store."

"Where did he come from?"

"I don't know."

"How many does he have in his family?"

"I don't know."

"What ticket does he vote?"

"I don't know."

"What church does he go to?"

"I don't know, and don't care. What are you asking all these questions for?"

If you had a store in Philadelphia would you answer me like that? If so, then you are conducting your business just as I carried on my father's business in Worthington, Massachusetts. You don't know where your neighbor came from when he moved to Philadelphia, and you don't care. If you had cared you would be a rich man now. If you had cared enough about him to take an interest in his affairs, to find out what he needed, you would have been rich. But you go through the world saying, "No opportunity to get rich," and there is the fault right at your own door.

Warrior Wisdom: the more you understand your market, the greater the opportunities you'll find in that market. Before you stretch yourself too thin in multiple markets, ask yourself whether you've fully "mined" the market you're currently in.

-Mike Agugliaro

But another young man gets up over there and says, "I cannot take up the mercantile business." (While I am talking of trade it applies to every occupation.)

"Why can't you go into the mercantile business?"

"Because I haven't any capital."

Oh, the weak and dudish creature that can't see over its collar! It makes a person weak to see these little dudes standing around the corners and saying, "Oh, if I had plenty of capital, how rich I would get."

"Young man, do you think you are going to get rich on capital?"

"Certainly."

Well, I say, "Certainly not."

If your mother has plenty of money, and she will set you up in business, you will "set her up in business," supplying you with capital.

The moment a young man or woman gets more money than he or she has grown to by practical experience, that moment he has gotten a curse. It is no help to a young man or woman to inherit money. It is no help to your children to leave them money, but if you leave them education, if you leave them Christian and noble character, if you leave them a wide circle of friends, if you leave them an honorable name, it is far better than that they should have money. It would be worse for them, worse for the nation, that they should have any money at all. Oh, young man, if you have inherited money, don't regard it as a help. It will curse you through your years, and deprive you of the very best things of human life. There is no class of people to be pitied so much as the inexperienced sons and daughters of the rich of our generation. I pity the rich man's son. He can never know the best things in life.

One of the best things in our life is when a young man has earned his own living, and when he becomes engaged to some lovely young woman, and makes up his mind to have a home of his own. Then with that same love comes also that divine inspiration toward better things, and he begins to save his money. He begins to leave off his bad habits and put money in the bank. When he has a few hundred dollars he goes out in the suburbs to look for a home. He goes to the savings-bank, perhaps, for half of the value, and then goes for his wife, and when he takes his bride over the threshold of that door for the first time he says in words of eloquence my voice can never touch: "I have earned this home myself. It is all mine, and I divide with thee." That is the grandest moment a human heart may ever know.

But a rich man's son can never know that. He takes his bride into a finer mansion, it may be, but he is obliged to go all the way through it and say to his wife, "My mother gave me that, my mother gave me that, and my mother gave me this," until his wife wishes she had married his mother. I pity the rich man's son.

Warrior Wisdom: your family and your employees will benefit from your success. But make sure you don't just reward them; you should also train them in the skills that made you successful.

-Mike Agugliaro

The statistics of Massachusetts showed that not one rich man's son out of seventeen ever dies rich. I pity the rich man's sons unless they have the good sense of the elder Vanderbilt, which sometimes happens. He went to his father and said, "Did you earn all your money?" "I did, my son. I began to work on a ferry-boat for twenty-five cents a day." "Then," said his son, "I will have none of your money," and he, too, tried to get employment on a ferry-boat that Saturday night. He could not get one there, but he did get a place for three dollars a week. Of course, if a rich man's son will do that, he will get the discipline of a poor boy that is worth more than a university education to any man. He would then be able to take care of the millions of his father. But as a rule the rich men will not let their sons do the very thing that made them great. As a rule, the rich man will not allow his son to work--and his mother! Why, she would think it was a social disgrace if her poor, weak, little lily-fingered, sissy sort of a boy had to earn his living with honest toil. I have no pity for such rich men's sons.

I remember one at Niagara Falls. I think I remember one a great deal nearer. I think there are gentlemen present who were at a great banquet, and I beg pardon of his friends. At a banquet here in Philadelphia there sat beside me a kind-hearted young man, and he said, "Mr. Conwell, you have been sick for two or three years. When you go out, take my limousine, and it will take you up to your house on Broad Street." I thanked him very much, and perhaps I ought not to mention the incident in this way, but I follow the facts. I got on to the seat with the driver of that limousine, outside, and when we were going up I asked the driver, "How much did this limousine cost?"

"Six thousand eight hundred, and he had to pay the duty on it."

"Well," I said, "does the owner of this machine ever drive it himself?" At that the chauffeur laughed so heartily that he lost control of his machine. He was so surprised at the question that he ran up on the sidewalk, and around a corner lamp-post out into the street again. And when he got out into the street he laughed till the whole machine trembled.

He said: "He drive this machine! Oh, he would be lucky if he knew enough to get out when we get there."

I must tell you about a rich man's son at Niagara Falls. I came in from the lecture to the hotel, and as I approached the desk of the clerk there stood a millionaire's son from New York. He was an indescribable specimen of anthropologic potency. He had a skull-cap on one side of his head, with a gold tassel in the top of it, and a gold-headed cane under his arm with more in it than in his head. It is a very difficult thing to describe that young man. He wore an eye-glass that he could not see through, patent-leather boots that he could not walk in, and pants that he could not sit down in--dressed like a grasshopper. This human cricket came up to the clerk's desk just as I entered, adjusted his unseeing eye-glass, and spake in this wise to the clerk. You see, he thought it was "Hinglish, you know," to lisp. "Thir, will you have the kindness to supply me with thome papah and enwelophs!" The hotel clerk measured that man quick, and he pulled the envelopes and paper out of a drawer, threw them across the counter toward the young man, and then turned away to his books. You should have seen that young man when those envelopes came across that counter. He swelled up like a gobbler turkey, adjusted his unseeing eye-glass, and yelled: "Come right back here. Now thir, will you order a thervant to take that papah and enwelophs to yondah dethk."

Oh, the poor, miserable, contemptible American monkey! He could not carry paper and envelopes twenty feet. I suppose he could not get his arms down to do it. I have no pity for such travesties upon human nature. If you have not capital, young man, I am glad of it. What you need is common sense, not copper cents.

The best thing I can do is to illustrate by actual facts well-known to you all. A. T. Stewart, a poor boy in New York, had $1.50 to begin life on. He lost 87

1/2 cents of that on the very first venture. How fortunate that young man who loses the first time he gambles. That boy said, "I will never gamble again in business," and he never did. How came he to lose 87 1/2 cents? You probably all know the story how he lost it--because he bought some needles, threads, and buttons to sell which people did not want, and had them left on his hands, a dead loss.

Said the boy, "I will not lose any more money in that way." Then he went around first to the doors and asked the people what they did want. Then when he had found out what they wanted he invested his 62 1/2 cents to supply a known demand. Study it wherever you choose--in business, in your profession, in your housekeeping, whatever your life, that one thing is the secret of success. You must first know the demand. You must first know what people need, and then invest yourself where you are most needed.

Warrior Wisdom: in your market, what do people need? What's in demand? What are the big problems to be solved? Answer that question (and keep asking and answering it regularly) and you have the key to limitless wealth.

-Mike Agugliaro

A. T. Stewart went on that principle until he was worth what amounted afterward to forty millions of dollars, owning the very store in which Mr. Wanamaker carries on his great work in New York. His fortune was made by his losing something, which taught him the great lesson that he must only invest himself or his money in something that people need. When will you salesmen learn it? When will you manufacturers learn that you must know the changing needs of humanity if you would succeed in life? Apply yourselves, all you Christian people, as manufacturers or merchants or workmen to supply that human need. It is a great principle as broad as humanity and as deep as the Scripture itself.

The best illustration I ever heard was of John Jacob Astor. You know that he made the money of the Astor family when he lived in New York. He came across the sea in debt for his fare. But that poor boy with nothing in his pocket made the fortune of the Astor family on one principle. Some young man here to-night will say, "Well they could make those fortunes over in New York but they could not do it in Philadelphia!" My friends, did you ever read that wonderful book of Riis (his memory is sweet to us because of his recent death), wherein is given his statistical account of the records taken in 1889 of 107 millionaires of New York. If you read the account you will see that out of the 107 millionaires only seven made their money in New York. Out of the 107 millionaires worth ten million dollars in real estate then, 67 of them made their money in towns of less than 3,500 inhabitants. The richest man in this country to-day, if you read the real-estate values, has never moved away from a town of 3,500 inhabitants. It makes not so much difference where you are as who you are. But if you cannot get rich in Philadelphia you certainly cannot do it in New York.

 **Warrior Wisdom**: in your business, you might be tempted by "greener pastures" (whether that is a new market to serve, or the employees you're trying to hire, or some other thing you assume is better elsewhere). Remember that opportunity exists everywhere for those Warriors who step up!
-Mike Agugliaro

Now John Jacob Astor illustrated what can be done anywhere. He had a mortgage once on a millinery-store, and they could not sell bonnets enough to pay the interest on his money. So he foreclosed that mortgage, took possession of the store, and went into partnership with the very same people, in the same store, with the same capital. He did not give them a dollar of capital. They had to sell goods to get any money. Then he left them alone in the store just as they had been before, and he went out and sat down on a bench in the park in the shade. What was John Jacob Astor doing out there, and in partnership with people who had failed on his own hands? He had the most important and, to my mind, the most pleasant part of that partnership on his hands. For as John Jacob Astor sat on that bench he was watching the ladies as they went by; and where is the man who would not get rich at that business? As he sat on the bench if a lady passed him with her shoulders back and head up, and looked straight to the front, as if she did not care if all the world did gaze on her, then he studied her bonnet, and by the time it was out of sight he knew the shape of the frame, the color of the trimmings, and the crinklings in the feather. I sometimes try to describe a bonnet, but not always. I would not try to describe a modern bonnet. Where is the man that could describe one? This aggregation of all sorts of driftwood stuck on the back of the head, or the side of the neck, like a rooster with only one tail feather left. But in John Jacob Astor's day there was some art about the millinery business, and he went to the millinery-store and said to them: "Now put into the show-window just such a bonnet as I describe to you, because I have already seen a lady who likes such a bonnet. Don't make up any more until I come back."

Then he went out and sat down again, and another lady passed him of a different form, of different complexion, with a different shape and color of bonnet. "Now," said he, "put such a bonnet as that in the show window." He did not fill his show-window up town with a lot of hats and bonnets to drive people away, and then sit on the back stairs and bawl because people went to Wanamaker's to trade. He did not have a hat or a bonnet in that show-window but what some lady liked before it was made up. The tide of custom began immediately to turn in, and that has been the foundation of the greatest store in New York in that line, and still exists as one of three stores. Its fortune was made by John Jacob Astor after they had failed in business, not by giving them any more money, but by finding out what the ladies liked for bonnets before they wasted any material in making them up. I tell you if a man could foresee the millinery business he could foresee anything under heaven!

Suppose I were to go through this audience to-night and ask you in this great manufacturing city if there are not opportunities to get rich in manufacturing. "Oh yes," some young man says, "there are opportunities here still if you build with some trust and if you have two or three millions of dollars to begin with as capital." Young man, the history of the breaking up of the trusts by that attack upon "big business" is only illustrating what is now the opportunity of the smaller man. The time never came in the history of the world when you could get rich so quickly manufacturing without capital as you can now.

But you will say, "You cannot do anything of the kind. You cannot start without capital." Young man, let me illustrate for a moment. I must do it. It is my duty to every young man and woman, because we are all going into business very soon on the same plan. Young man, remember if you know what people need you have gotten more knowledge of a fortune than any amount of capital can give you.

Warrior Wisdom: lack of capital is a huge limiting belief. What other limiting beliefs are holding you back? As you read this story, consider how it applies to your life – perhaps you think capital (or some other thing) is holding you back.
-Mike Agugliaro

There was a poor man out of work living in Hingham, Massachusetts. He lounged around the house until one day his wife told him to get out and work, and, as he lived in Massachusetts, he obeyed his wife. He went out and sat down on the shore of the bay, and whittled a soaked shingle into a wooden chain. His children that evening quarreled over it, and he whittled a second one to keep peace. While he was whittling the second one a neighbor came in and said: "Why don't you whittle toys and sell them? You could make money at that." "Oh," he said, "I would not know what to make." "Why don't you ask your own children right here in your own house what to make?" "What is the use of trying that?" said the carpenter. "My children are different from other people's children." (I used to see people like that when I taught school.) But he acted upon the hint, and the next morning when Mary came down the stairway, he asked, "What do you want for a toy?" She began to tell him she would like a doll's bed, a doll's washstand, a doll's carriage, a little doll's umbrella, and went on with a list of things that would take him a lifetime to supply. So, consulting his own children, in his own house, he took the firewood, for he had no money to buy lumber, and whittled those strong, unpainted Hingham toys that were for so many years known all over the world. That man began to make those toys for his own children, and then made copies and sold them through the boot-and-shoe store next door. He began to make a little money, and then a little more, and Mr. Lawson, in his _Frenzied Finance_ says that man is the richest man in old Massachusetts, and I think it is the truth. And that man is worth a hundred millions of dollars to-day, and has been only thirty-four years making it on that one principle-- that one must judge that what his own children like at home other people's children would like in their homes, too; to judge the human heart by oneself, by one's wife or by one's children. It is the royal road to success in manufacturing. "Oh," but you say, "didn't he have any capital?" Yes, a penknife, but I don't know that he had paid for that.

Warrior Wisdom: not sure how to invest in your business to grow? It's simple – find out what your customers want and need, and figure out how you can deliver it.

-Mike Agugliaro

I spoke thus to an audience in New Britain, Connecticut, and a lady four seats back went home and tried to take off her collar, and the collar-button stuck in the buttonhole. She threw it out and said, "I am going to get up something better than that to put on collars." Her husband said: "After what Conwell said to-night, you see there is a need of an improved collar-fastener that is easier to handle. There is a human need; there is a great fortune. Now, then, get up a collar-button and get rich." He made fun of her, and consequently made fun of me, and that is one of the saddest things which comes over me like a deep cloud of midnight sometimes--although I have worked so hard for more than half a century, yet how little I have ever really done. Notwithstanding the greatness and the handsomeness of your compliment to-night, I do not believe there is one in ten of you that is going to make a million of dollars because you are here to-night; but it is not my fault, it is yours. I say that sincerely. What is the use of my talking if people never do what I advise them to do? When her husband ridiculed her, she made up her mind she would make a better collar-button, and when a woman makes up her mind "she will," and does not say anything about it, she does it. It was that New England woman who invented the snap button which you can find anywhere now. It was first a collar-button with a spring cap attached to the outer side. Any of you who wear modern waterproofs know the button that simply pushes together, and when you unbutton it you simply pull it apart. That is the button to which I refer, and which she invented. She afterward invented several other buttons, and then invested in more, and then was taken into partnership with great factories. Now that woman goes over the sea every summer in her private steamship--yes, and takes her husband with her! If her husband were to die, she would have money enough left now to buy a foreign duke or count or some such title as that at the latest quotations.

Now what is my lesson in that incident? It is this: I told her then, though I did not know her, what I now say to you, "Your wealth is too near to you. You are looking right over it"; and she had to look over it because it was right under her chin.

Warrior Wisdom: this is such a powerful lesson and it applies to you! There is money right under your chin if you would only look!

-Mike Agugliaro

I have read in the newspaper that a woman never invented anything. Well, that newspaper ought to begin again. Of course, I do not refer to gossip--I refer to machines--and if I did I might better include the men. That newspaper could never appear if women had not invented something. Friends, think. Ye women, think! You say you cannot make a fortune because you are in some laundry, or running a sewing-machine, it may be, or walking before some loom, and yet you can be a millionaire if you will but follow this almost infallible direction.

When you say a woman doesn't invent anything, I ask, Who invented the Jacquard loom that wove every stitch you wear? Mrs. Jacquard. The printer's roller, the printing-press, were invented by farmers' wives.

Who invented the cotton-gin of the South that enriched our country so amazingly? Mrs. General Greene invented the cotton-gin and showed the idea to Mr. Whitney, and he, like a man, seized it. Who was it that invented the sewing-machine? If I would go to school to-morrow and ask your children they would say, "Elias Howe."

He was in the Civil War with me, and often in my tent, and I often heard him say that he worked fourteen years to get up that sewing-machine. But his wife made up her mind one day that they would starve to death if there wasn't something or other invented pretty soon, and so in two hours she invented the sewing-machine. Of course he took out the patent in his name. Men always do that. Who was it that invented the mower and the reaper? According to Mr. McCormick's confidential communication, so recently published, it was a West Virginia woman, who, after his father and he had failed altogether in making a reaper and gave it up, took a lot of shears and nailed them together on the edge of a board, with one shaft of each pair loose, and then wired them so that when she pulled the wire one way it closed them, and when she pulled the wire the other way it opened them, and there she had the principle of the mowing-machine. If you look at a mowing-machine, you will see it is nothing but a lot of shears. If a woman can invent a mowing-machine, if a woman can invent a Jacquard loom, if a woman can invent a cotton-gin, if a woman can invent a trolley switch--as she did and made the trolleys possible; if a woman can invent, as Mr. Carnegie said, the great iron squeezers that laid the foundation of all the steel millions of the United States, "we men" can invent anything under the stars! I say that for the encouragement of the men.

Who are the great inventors of the world? Again this lesson comes before us. The great inventor sits next to you, or you are the person yourself.

 **Warrior Wisdom**: this isn't really about men and women – it's about unexpected innovators. Do you think of yourself as an innovator in your industry? Most wouldn't dare think of themselves that way but what would be possible if you did?
-Mike Agugliaro

"Oh," but you will say, "I have never invented anything in my life." Neither did the great inventors until they discovered one great secret. Do you think it is a man with a head like a bushel measure or a man like a stroke of lightning? It is neither. The really great man is a plain, straightforward, everyday, common-sense man. You would not dream that he was a great inventor if you did not see something he had actually done. His neighbors do not regard him so great. You never see anything great over your back fence. You say there is no greatness among your neighbors. It is all away off somewhere else. Their greatness is ever so simple, so plain, so earnest, so practical, that the neighbors and friends never recognize it.

True greatness is often unrecognized. That is sure. You do not know anything about the greatest men and women.

 **Warrior Wisdom**: history's greatest people achieved their success, fame, and historical permanence because they stepped up when it was required of them. If you are reading this, it's required of you as well! Your family and your employees need you to be great. Step up!

-Mike Agugliaro

I went out to write the life of General Garfield, and a neighbor, knowing I was in a hurry, and as there was a great crowd around the front door, took me around to General Garfield's back door and shouted, "Jim! Jim!" And very soon "Jim" came to the door and let me in, and I wrote the biography of one of the grandest men of the nation, and yet he was just the same old "Jim" to his neighbor. If you know a great man in Philadelphia and you should meet him to-morrow, you would say, "How are you, Sam?" or "Good morning, Jim." Of course you would. That is just what you would do.

One of my soldiers in the Civil War had been sentenced to death, and I went up to the White House in Washington--sent there for the first time in my life to see the President. I went into the waiting-room and sat down with a lot of others on the benches, and the secretary asked one after another to tell him what they wanted. After the secretary had been through the line, he went in, and then came back to the door and motioned for me. I went up to that anteroom, and the secretary said: "That is the President's door right over there. Just rap on it and go right in." I never was so taken aback, friends, in all my life, never. The secretary himself made it worse for me, because he had told me how to go in and then went out another door to the left and shut that.

There I was, in the hallway by myself before the President of the United States of America's door. I had been on fields of battle, where the shells did sometimes shriek and the bullets did sometimes hit me, but I always wanted to run. I have no sympathy with the old man who says, "I would just as soon march up to the cannon's mouth as eat my dinner." I have no faith in a man who doesn't know enough to be afraid when he is being shot at. I never was so afraid when the shells came around us at Antietam as I was when I went into that room that day; but I finally mustered the courage--I don't know how I ever did--and at arm's-length tapped on the door. The man inside did not help me at all, but yelled out, "Come in and sit down!"

Well, I went in and sat down on the edge of a chair, and wished I were in Europe, and the man at the table did not look up. He was one of the world's greatest men, and was made great by one single rule. Oh, that all the young people of Philadelphia were before me now and I could say just this one thing, and that they would remember it. I would give a lifetime for the effect it would have on our city and on civilization. Abraham Lincoln's principle for greatness can be adopted by nearly all. This was his rule: Whatsoever he had to do at all, he put his whole mind into it and held it all there until that was all done.

Warrior Wisdom: *"Whatsoever he had to do at all, he put his whole mind into it and held it all there until that was all done."* Make that your daily practice at every task and you will be amazed at the results!

-Mike Agugliaro

That makes men great almost anywhere. He stuck to those papers at that table and did not look up at me, and I sat there trembling. Finally, when he had put the string around his papers, he pushed them over to one side and looked over to me, and a smile came over his worn face. He said: "I am a very busy man and have only a few minutes to spare. Now tell me in the fewest words what it is you want." I began to tell him, and mentioned the case, and he said: "I have heard all about it and you do not need to say any more. Mr. Stanton was talking to me only a few days ago about that. You can go to the hotel and rest assured that the President never did sign an order to shoot a boy under twenty years of age, and never will. You can say that to his mother anyhow."

Then he said to me, "How is it going in the field?" I said, "We sometimes get discouraged." And he said: "It is all right. We are going to win out now. We are getting very near the light. No man ought to wish to be President of the United States, and I will be glad when I get through; then Tad and I are going out to Springfield, Illinois. I have bought a farm out there and I don't

40

care if I again earn only twenty-five cents a day. Tad has a mule team, and we are going to plant onions."

Then he asked me, "Were you brought up on a farm?" I said, "Yes; in the Berkshire Hills of Massachusetts." He then threw his leg over the corner of the big chair and said, "I have heard many a time, ever since I was young, that up there in those hills you have to sharpen the noses of the sheep in order to get down to the grass between the rocks." He was so familiar, so everyday, so farmer-like, that I felt right at home with him at once.

He then took hold of another roll of paper, and looked up at me and said, "Good morning." I took the hint then and got up and went out. After I had gotten out I could not realize I had seen the President of the United States at all. But a few days later, when still in the city, I saw the crowd pass through the East Room by the coffin of Abraham Lincoln, and when I looked at the upturned face of the murdered President I felt then that the man I had seen such a short time before, who, so simple a man, so plain a man, was one of the greatest men that God ever raised up to lead a nation on to ultimate liberty. Yet he was only "Old Abe" to his neighbors. When they had the second funeral, I was invited among others, and went out to see that same coffin put back in the tomb at Springfield. Around the tomb stood Lincoln's old neighbors, to whom he was just "Old Abe." Of course that is all they would say.

Did you ever see a man who struts around altogether too large to notice an ordinary working mechanic? Do you think he is great? He is nothing but a puffed-up balloon, held down by his big feet. There is no greatness there.

Who are the great men and women? My attention was called the other day to the history of a very little thing that made the fortune of a very poor man. It was an awful thing, and yet because of that experience he--not a great inventor or genius--invented the pin that now is called the safety-pin, and out of that safety-pin made the fortune of one of the great aristocratic families of this nation.

A poor man in Massachusetts who had worked in the nail-works was injured at thirty-eight, and he could earn but little money. He was employed in the office to rub out the marks on the bills made by pencil memorandums, and he used a rubber until his hand grew tired. He then tied a piece of rubber on the end of a stick and worked it like a plane. His little girl came and said, "Why, you have a patent, haven't you?" The father said afterward, "My daughter told me when I took that stick and put the rubber on the end that there was a patent, and that was the first thought of that." He went to Boston and applied for his patent, and every one of you that has a rubber-tipped pencil in your pocket is now paying tribute to the millionaire. No capital, not a penny did he invest in it. All was income, all the way up into the millions.

But let me hasten to one other greater thought. "Show me the great men and women who live in Philadelphia." A gentleman over there will get up and say: "We don't have any great men in Philadelphia. They don't live here. They live away off in Rome or St. Petersburg or London or Manayunk, or anywhere else but here in our town." I have come now to the apex of my thought. I have come now to the heart of the whole matter and to the center of my struggle: Why isn't Philadelphia a greater city in its greater wealth? Why does New York excel Philadelphia? People say, "Because of her harbor." Why do many other cities of the United States get ahead of Philadelphia now? There is only one answer, and that is because our own people talk down their own city. If there ever was a community on earth that has to be forced ahead, it is the city of Philadelphia. If we are to have a boulevard, talk it down; if we are going to have better schools, talk them down; if you wish to have wise legislation, talk it down; talk all the proposed improvements down. That is the only great wrong that I can lay at the feet of the magnificent Philadelphia that has been so universally kind to me. I say it is time we turn around in our city and begin to talk up the things that are in our city, and begin to set them before the world as the people of Chicago, New York, St. Louis, and San Francisco do. Oh, if we only could get that spirit out among our people, that we can do things in Philadelphia and do them well!

Warrior Wisdom: what is written here about Philadelphia is true of your business as well. You make your own reality. If you get caught up in the problems and challenges in your business, that negative viewpoint will come to define your business (which, in turn, will impact your attitude, your productivity, your hiring practices, your sales, your service, and even your health). Remember this: you make your own reality. Talk down your challenges and talk up your accomplishments and opportunities.

-Mike Agugliaro

Arise, ye millions of Philadelphians, trust in God and man, and believe in the great opportunities that are right here not over in New York or Boston, but here--for business, for everything that is worth living for on earth. There was never an opportunity greater. Let us talk up our own city.

But there are two other young men here to-night, and that is all I will venture to say, because it is too late. One over there gets up and says, "There is going to be a great man in Philadelphia, but never was one."

"Oh, is that so? When are you going to be great?"

"When I am elected to some political office." Young man, won't you learn a lesson in the primer of politics that it is a *prima facie* evidence of littleness to hold office under our form of government? Great men get into office sometimes, but what this country needs is men that will do what we tell them to do.

Warrior Wisdom: actions, not words, are the purest form of greatness. If you want to be great, ACT great in all aspects of your life and business.
                                                        -Mike Agugliaro

This nation--where the people rule--is governed by the people, for the people, and so long as it is, then the office-holder is but the servant of the people, and the Bible says the servant cannot be greater than the master. The Bible says, "He that is sent cannot be greater than Him who sent Him." The people rule, or should rule, and if they do, we do not need the greater men in office. If the great men in America took our offices, we would change to an empire in the next ten years.

I know of a great many young women, now that woman's suffrage is coming, who say, "I am going to be President of the United States some day."I believe in woman's suffrage, and there is no doubt but what it is coming, and I am getting out of the way, anyhow. I may want an office by and by myself; but if the ambition for an office influences the women in their desire to vote, I want to say right here what I say to the young men, that if you only get the privilege of casting one vote, you don't get anything that is worth while. Unless you can control more than one vote, you will be unknown, and your influence so dissipated as practically not to be felt. This country is not run by votes. Do you think it is? It is governed by influence. It is governed by the ambitions and the enterprises which control votes. The young woman that thinks she is going to vote for the sake of holding an office is making an awful blunder.

That other young man gets up and says, "There are going to be great men in this country and in Philadelphia."

"Is that so? When?"

"When there comes a great war, when we get into difficulty through watchful waiting in Mexico; when we get into war with England over some frivolous deed, or with Japan or China or New Jersey or some distant country. Then I will march up to the cannon's mouth; I will sweep up among the glistening bayonets; I will leap into the arena and tear down the flag and bear it away in triumph. I will come home with stars on my shoulder, and hold every office in the gift of the nation, and I will be great." No, you won't. You think you are going to be made great by an office, but remember that if you are not great before you get the office, you won't be great when you secure it. It will only be a burlesque in that shape.

We had a Peace Jubilee here after the Spanish War. Out West they don't believe this, because they said, "Philadelphia would not have heard of any Spanish War until fifty years hence." Some of you saw the procession go up Broad Street. I was away, but the family wrote to me that the tally-ho coach with Lieutenant Hobson upon it stopped right at the front door and the people shouted, "Hurrah for Hobson!" and if I had been there I would have yelled too, because he deserves much more of his country than he has ever received. But suppose I go into school and say, "Who sunk the _Merrimac_ at Santiago?" and if the boys answer me, "Hobson," they will tell me seven-eighths of a lie. There were seven other heroes on that steamer, and they, by virtue of their position, were continually exposed to the Spanish fire, while Hobson, as an officer, might reasonably be behind the smoke-stack. You have gathered in this house your most intelligent people, and yet, perhaps, not one here can name the other seven men.

We ought not to so teach history. We ought to teach that, however humble a man's station may be, if he does his full duty in that place he is just as much entitled to the American people's honor as is the king upon his throne. But we do not so teach. We are now teaching everywhere that the generals do all the fighting.

I remember that, after the war, I went down to see General Robert E. Lee, that magnificent Christian gentleman of whom both North and South are now proud as one of our great Americans. The general told me about his servant, "Rastus," who was an enlisted colored soldier. He called him in one day to make fun of him, and said, "Rastus, I hear that all the rest of your company are killed, and why are you not killed?" Rastus winked at him and said, "'Cause when there is any fightin' goin' on I stay back with the generals."

I remember another illustration. I would leave it out but for the fact that when you go to the library to read this lecture, you will find this has been printed in it for twenty-five years. I shut my eyes--shut them close--and lo! I see the faces of my youth. Yes, they sometimes say to me, "Your hair is not white; you are working night and day without seeming ever to stop; you can't be old." But when I shut my eyes, like any other man of my years, oh, then come trooping back the faces of the loved and lost of long ago, and I know, whatever men may say, it is evening-time.

I shut my eyes now and look back to my native town in Massachusetts, and I see the cattle-show ground on the mountain-top; I can see the horse-sheds there. I can see the Congregational church; see the town hall and mountaineers' cottages; see a great assembly of people turning out, dressed resplendently, and I can see flags flying and handkerchiefs waving and hear bands playing. I can see that company of soldiers that had re-enlisted marching up on that cattle-show ground. I was but a boy, but I was captain of that company and puffed out with pride. A cambric needle would have burst me all to pieces. Then I thought it was the greatest event that ever came to man on earth. If you have ever thought you would like to be a king or queen, you go and be received by the mayor.

The bands played, and all the people turned out to receive us. I marched up that Common so proud at the head of my troops, and we turned down into the town hall. Then they seated my soldiers down the center aisle and I sat down on the front seat. A great assembly of people a hundred or two-- came in to fill the town hall, so that they stood up all around. Then the town officers came in and formed a half-circle. The mayor of the town sat in the middle of the platform. He was a man who had never held office before; but he was a good man, and his friends have told me that I might use this without giving them offense. He was a good man, but he thought an office made a man great. He came up and took his seat, adjusted his powerful spectacles, and looked around, when he suddenly spied me sitting there on the front seat. He came right forward on the platform and invited me up to sit with the town officers. No town officer ever took any notice of me before I went to war, except to advise the teacher to thrash me, and now I was invited up on the stand with the town officers. Oh my! the town mayor was then the emperor, the king of our day and our time. As I came up on the platform they gave me a chair about this far, I would say, from the front.

When I had got seated, the chairman of the Selectmen arose and came forward to the table, and we all supposed he would introduce the Congregational minister, who was the only orator in town, and that he would give the oration to the returning soldiers. But, friends, you should have seen the surprise which ran over the audience when they discovered that the old fellow was going to deliver that speech himself. He had never made a speech in his life, but he fell into the same error that hundreds of other men have fallen into. It seems so strange that a man won't learn he must speak his piece as a boy if he in-tends to be an orator when he is grown, but he seems to think all he has to do is to hold an office to be a great orator.

 **Warrior Wisdom**: your team doesn't need you to be the smartest or best speaker – you just need to lead them with power.

-Mike Agugliaro

So he came up to the front, and brought with him a speech which he had learned by heart walking up and down the pasture, where he had frightened the cattle. He brought the manuscript with him and spread it out on the table so as to be sure he might see it. He adjusted his spectacles and leaned over it for a moment and marched back on that platform, and then came forward like this--tramp, tramp, tramp. He must have studied the subject a great deal, when you come to think of it, because he assumed an "elocutionary" attitude. He rested heavily upon his left heel, threw back his shoulders, slightly advanced the right foot, opened the organs of speech, and advanced his right foot at an angle of forty-five. As he stood in that elocutionary attitude, friends, this is just the way that speech went. Some people say to me, "Don't you exaggerate?" That would be impossible. But I am here for the lesson and not for the story, and this is the way it went:

"Fellow-citizens--" As soon as he heard his voice his fingers began to go like that, his knees began to shake, and then he trembled all over. He choked and swallowed and came around to the table to look at the manuscript. Then he gathered himself up with clenched fists and came back: "Fellow-citizens, we are Fellow-citizens, we are--we are—we are--we are--we are--we are very happy--we are very happy--we are very happy. We are very happy to welcome back to their native town these soldiers who have fought and bled--and come back again to their native town. We are especially--we are especially--we are especially. We are especially pleased to see with us to-day this young hero" (that meant me)--"this young hero who in imagination" (friends, remember he said that; if he had not said "in imagination" I would not be egotistic enough to refer to it at all)--"this young hero who in imagination we have seen leading--we have seen leading--leading. We have seen leading his troops on to the deadly breach. We have seen his shining--we have seen his shining--his shining--his shining sword--flashing. Flashing in the sunlight, as he shouted to his troops, 'Come on'!"

Oh dear, dear, dear! how little that good man knew about war. If he had known anything about war at all he ought to have known what any of my G. A. R. comrades here to-night will tell you is true, that it is next to a crime for an officer of infantry ever in time of danger to go ahead of his men. "I, with my shining sword flashing in the sunlight, shouting to my troops, 'Come on'!" I never did it. Do you suppose I would get in front of my men to be shot in front by the enemy and in the back by my own men? That is no place for an officer. The place for the officer in actual battle is behind the line. How often, as a staff officer, I rode down the line, when our men were suddenly called to the line of battle, and the Rebel yells were coming out of the woods, and shouted: "Officers to the rear! Officers to the rear!" Then every officer gets behind the line of private soldiers, and the higher the officer's rank the farther behind he goes. Not because he is any the less brave, but because the laws of war require that.

 **Warrior Wisdom**: you once worked on the front lines of your industry and now you might be struggling to make the adjustment to lead your team. But if you want to own a service business, it's time to change your mindset. Your team needs you directing them from a higher vantage point.
-Mike Agugliaro

And yet he shouted, "I, with my shining sword--" In that house there sat the company of my soldiers who had carried that boy across the Carolina rivers that he might not wet his feet. Some of them had gone far out to get a pig or a chicken. Some of them had gone to death under the shell-swept pines in the mountains of Tennessee, yet in the good man's speech they were scarcely known. He did refer to them, but only incidentally. The hero of the hour was this boy. Did the nation owe him anything? No, nothing then and nothing now. Why was he the hero? Simply because that man fell into that same human error--that this boy was great because he was an officer and these were only private soldiers.

Oh, I learned the lesson then that I will never forget so long as the tongue of the bell of time continues to swing for me. Greatness consists not in the holding of some future office, but really consists in doing great deeds with little means and the accomplishment of vast purposes from the private ranks of life.

 **Warrior Wisdom**: Warriors step up to the challenge and privilege of greatness. If you want to be successful in your business, it's time to step up to greatness.
-Mike Agugliaro

To be great at all one must be great here, now, in Philadelphia. He who can give to this city better streets and better sidewalks, better schools and more colleges, more happiness and more civilization, more of God, he will be great anywhere. Let every man or woman here, if you never hear me again, remember this, that if you wish to be great at all, you must begin where you are and what you are, in Philadelphia, now. He that can give to his city any blessing, he who can be a good citizen while he lives here, he that can make better homes, he that can be a blessing whether he works in the shop or sits behind the counter or keeps house, whatever be his life, he who would be great anywhere must first be great in his own Philadelphia.

Applying These Timeless Secrets Today – By Mike Agugliaro

As a service business owner, it's your job to grow your business. It's your job to lead your team to greatness. Unfortunately, many service business owners get caught up with the challenges and problems in their own business and look to what they believe are greener pastures – "if only there was a better market," or, "if only I had better customers," or, "if only all the good employees weren't taken," and so on. What they fail to realize is that they have acres of diamonds right in their own business – profit, people, customers, marketing, tradelines, and more. All it takes is to recognize that there are opportunities and then to chase after them relentlessly. And, once you realize there are opportunities in your own your business, you'll start seeing them everywhere!

It all starts with your mindset: start looking at things differently, shed your limiting beliefs, and don't let a lack of capital hold you back. Then listen to your market and see what problems they have and start solving those. Be great and lead your team to greatness.

You are sitting on acres of diamonds – on a mountain of untapped fortune. Now start mining it.

Take Action!

__ What are the diamonds in your business and how do you value them? (i.e. another service line: $250K; reach out to customers more each year: $200K; change my mindset: $10 million; etc.)

_____

_____

_____

__ What limiting beliefs do you have?

_____

_____

_____

__ What struggles do you encounter while leading your team?

_____

_____

__ Putting aside your limiting beliefs, how can you be truly GREAT?

_____

_____

__ What are the problems and challenges that your marketplace is asking for?

_____

_____

__ What lessons stood out for you while reading this?

_____

_____

__ Stop doing actions (Actions you currently do now but should stop doing)

_____

_____

__ Keep doing actions (Actions you currently do now and should keep doing)

_____

_____

__ Start doing actions (Actions you don't do now but should start doing)

_____

_____

__ Who will do new actions? (Assign the action to yourself or someone else)

_____

_____

___ By when? (When will these actions be complete?)

_____

_____

___ What is the outcome you desire after applying these lessons?

_____

_____

THE ART OF MONEY-GETTING

Introduction By Mike Agugliaro

Phineas Taylor Barnum is best knowns as P. T. Barnum. He lived from 1810 to 1891 and is famous for operating the Barnum and Bailey Circus. But don't disregard him because you're thinking of clowns and elephants, or because you can't make the connection to your service business.

Ultimately, P. T. Barnum was a business owner. In his twenties he started a business AND founded a newspaper. Later he started a theater and a museum. He was an author and a publisher. One of his theatrical businesses paid an entertainer $1,000 a night for 150 nights in a row. (This is $1,000 in the 1850's! According to one purchasing power calculator, that's the modern equivalent of at least $30,000... each and every night.) So trust me when I tell you: you don't want to dismiss P. T. Barnum because you think of him as a circus owner!

Barnum was a business owner and he knew how to find customers, attract them into his business, and earn money from them. Although his circus from the 1800's and your service business from 150 years later might seem different, many of the fundamental concepts haven't changed.

In fact, as you read Barnum's writing below, you'll see how many of his foundational money-making concepts are still so relevant today.

As you read this, pay attention to the following:

- Consider how the various trades of his day might differ from the trades of today but the information remains the same!
- Notice what he has to say about tobacco-chewing (and think about other habits you might have and how they affect you and those around you).
- Focus, perseverance, hard work – these are just as true today, and just as relevant to you and your team as they were 150 years ago when Barnum ran his circus.

Read Barnum's short writing with a pen in hand and take note of what he has to say. There's A LOT of gold in here.

The Art Of Money-Getting By P. T. Barnum

In the United States, where we have more land than people, it is not at all difficult for persons in good health to make money. In this comparatively new field there are so many avenues of success open, so many vocations which are not crowded, that any person of either sex who is willing, at least for the time being, to engage in any respectable occupation that offers, may find lucrative employment.

Those who really desire to attain an independence, have only to set their minds upon it, and adopt the proper means, as they do in regard to any other object which they wish to accomplish, and the thing is easily done.

Warrior Wisdom: there are unlimited opportunities to make money.

-Mike Agugliaro

But however easy it may be found to make money, I have no doubt many of my hearers will agree it is the most difficult thing in the world to keep it. The road to wealth is, as Dr. Franklin truly says, "as plain as the road to the mill." It consists simply in expending less than we earn; that seems to be a very simple problem. Mr. Micawber, one of those happy creations of the genial Dickens, puts the case in a strong light when he says that to have annual income of twenty pounds per annum, and spend twenty pounds and sixpence, is to be the most miserable of men; whereas, to have an income of only twenty pounds, and spend but nineteen pounds and sixpence is to be the happiest of mortals. Many of my readers may say, "we understand this: this is economy, and we know economy is wealth; we know we can't eat our cake and keep it also." Yet I beg to say that perhaps more cases of failure arise from mistakes on this point than almost any other. The fact is, many people think they understand economy when they really do not.

True economy is misapprehended, and people go through life without properly comprehending what that principle is. One says, "I have an income of so much, and here is my neighbor who has the same; yet every year he gets something ahead and I fall short; why is it? I know all about economy." He thinks he does, but he does not. There are men who think that economy consists in saving cheese-parings and candle-ends, in cutting off two pence from the laundress' bill and doing all sorts of little, mean, dirty things. Economy is not meanness. The misfortune is, also, that this class of persons let their economy apply in only one direction. They fancy they are so wonderfully economical in saving a half-penny where they ought to spend twopence, that they think they can afford to squander in other directions.

 Warrior Wisdom: don't focus on the little things when you should be spending more time on the big things. This is true of saving money, as discussed above, but about so many other factors in business as well!

-Mike Agugliaro

A few years ago, before kerosene oil was discovered or thought of, one might stop overnight at almost any farmer's house in the agricultural districts and get a very good supper, but after supper he might attempt to read in the sitting-room, and would find it impossible with the inefficient light of one candle. The hostess, seeing his dilemma, would say: "It is rather difficult to read here evenings; the proverb says 'you must have a ship at sea in order to be able to burn two candles at once;' we never have an extra candle except on extra occasions." These extra occasions occur, perhaps, twice a year. In this way the good woman saves five, six, or ten dollars in that time: but the information which might be derived from having the extra light would, of course, far outweigh a ton of candles.

But the trouble does not end here. Feeling that she is so economical in tallow candies, she thinks she can afford to go frequently to the village and spend twenty or thirty dollars for ribbons and furbelows, many of which are not necessary. This false connote may frequently be seen in men of business, and in those instances it often runs to writing-paper. You find good businessmen who save all the old envelopes and scraps, and would not tear a new sheet of paper, if they could avoid it, for the world. This is all very well; they may in this way save five or ten dollars a year, but being so economical (only in note paper), they think they can afford to waste time; to have expensive parties, and to drive their carriages. This is an illustration of Dr. Franklin's "saving at the spigot and wasting at the bung-hole;" "penny wise and pound foolish." Punch in speaking of this "one idea" class of people says "they are like the man who bought a penny herring for his family's dinner and then hired a coach and four to take it home." I never knew a man to succeed by practising this kind of economy.

Warrior Wisdom: this is a major problem today – people are spending more money than they make. How are you handling your money?

-Mike Agugliaro

True economy consists in always making the income exceed the out-go. Wear the old clothes a little longer if necessary; dispense with the new pair of gloves; mend the old dress: live on plainer food if need be; so that, under all circumstances, unless some unforeseen accident occurs, there will be a margin in favor of the income. A penny here, and a dollar there, placed at interest, goes on accumulating, and in this way the desired result is attained. It requires some training, perhaps, to accomplish this economy, but when once used to it, you will find there is more satisfaction in rational saving than in irrational spending.

Warrior Wisdom: *"It requires some training, perhaps, to accomplish this economy, but when once used to it, you will find there is more satisfaction in rational saving than in irrational spending."* I'm not advocating that you be stingy. Rather, I'm urging you to know what your income is and what your expenses are and to keep them both under firm control.

-Mike Agugliaro

Here is a recipe which I recommend: I have found it to work an excellent cure for extravagance, and especially for mistaken economy: When you find that you have no surplus at the end of the year, and yet have a good income, I advise you to take a few sheets of paper and form them into a book and mark down every item of expenditure. Post it every day or week in two columns, one headed "necessaries" or even "comforts", and the other headed "luxuries," and you will find that the latter column will be double, treble, and frequently ten times greater than the former.

Warrior Wisdom: what can be measured is managed. Track everything if you want to know the truth about anything.

-Mike Agugliaro

The real comforts of life cost but a small portion of what most of us can earn. Dr. Franklin says "it is the eyes of others and not our own eyes which ruin us. If all the world were blind except myself I should not care for fine clothes or furniture." It is the fear of what Mrs. Grundy may say that keeps the noses of many worthy families to the grindstone. In America many persons like to repeat "we are all free and equal," but it is a great mistake in more senses than one.

That we are born "free and equal" is a glorious truth in one sense, yet we are not all born equally rich, and we never shall be. One may say; "there is a man who has an income of fifty thousand dollars per annum, while I have but one thousand dollars; I knew that fellow when he was poor like myself; now he is rich and thinks he is better than I am; I will show him that I am as good as he is; I will go and buy a horse and buggy; no, I cannot do that, but I will go and hire one and ride this afternoon on the same road that he does, and thus prove to him that I am as good as he is."

Warrior Wisdom: many of our decisions are built around how we want to be perceived. When you stop caring what others think of you, you'll achieve a level of freedom to pursue what really matters in life.

-Mike Agugliaro

My friend, you need not take that trouble; you can easily prove that you are "as good as he is;" you have only to behave as well as he does; but you cannot make anybody believe that you are rich as he is. Besides, if you put on these "airs," add waste your time and spend your money, your poor wife will be obliged to scrub her fingers off at home, and buy her tea two ounces at a time, and everything else in proportion, in order that you may keep up "appearances," and, after all, deceive nobody. On the other hand, Mrs. Smith may say that her next-door neighbor married Johnson for his money, and "everybody says so." She has a nice one-thousand dollar camel's hair shawl, and she will make Smith get her an imitation one, and she will sit in a pew right next to her neighbor in church, in order to prove that she is her equal.

My good woman, you will not get ahead in the world, if your vanity and envy thus take the lead. In this country, where we believe the majority ought to rule, we ignore that principle in regard to fashion, and let a handful of people, calling themselves the aristocracy, run up a false standard of perfection, and in endeavoring to rise to that standard, we constantly keep ourselves poor; all the time digging away for the sake of outside appearances. How much wiser to be a "law unto ourselves" and say, "we will regulate our out-go by our income, and lay up something for a rainy day." People ought to be as sensible on the subject of money-getting as on any other subject. Like causes produces like effects. You cannot accumulate a fortune by taking the road that leads to poverty. It needs no prophet to tell us that those who live fully up to their means, without any thought of a reverse in this life, can never attain a pecuniary independence.

Warrior Wisdom: wealth and freedom are possible but only if you gain mastery over the things that threaten wealth and freedom.
                                            -Mike Agugliaro

Men and women accustomed to gratify every whim and caprice, will find it hard, at first, to cut down their various unnecessary expenses, and will feel it a great self-denial to live in a smaller house than they have been accustomed to, with less expensive furniture, less company, less costly clothing, fewer servants, a less number of balls, parties, theater-goings, carriage-ridings, pleasure excursions, cigar-smokings, liquor-drinkings, and other extravagances; but, after all, if they will try the plan of laying by a "nest-egg," or, in other words, a small sum of money, at interest or judiciously invested in land, they will be surprised at the pleasure to be derived from constantly adding to their little "pile," as well as from all the economical habits which are engendered by this course.

Warrior Wisdom: what are your "guilty pleasures" that are costing you wealth and freedom?
                                            -Mike Agugliaro

The old suit of clothes, and the old bonnet and dress, will answer for another season; the Croton or spring water taste better than champagne; a cold bath and a brisk walk will prove more exhilarating than a ride in the finest coach; a social chat, an evening's reading in the family circle, or an hour's play of "hunt the slipper" and "blind man's buff" will be far more pleasant than a fifty or five hundred dollar party, when the reflection on the difference in cost is indulged in by those who begin to know the pleasures of saving. Thousands of men are kept poor, and tens of thousands are made so after they have acquired quite sufficient to support them well through life, in consequence of laying their plans of living on too broad a platform. Some families expend twenty thousand dollars per annum, and some much more, and would scarcely know how to live on less, while others secure more solid enjoyment frequently on a twentieth part of that amount. Prosperity is a more severe ordeal than adversity, especially sudden prosperity. "Easy come, easy go," is an old and true proverb. A spirit of pride and vanity, when permitted to have full sway, is the undying canker-worm which gnaws the very vitals of a man's worldly possessions, let them be small or great, hundreds, or millions. Many persons, as they begin to prosper, immediately expand their ideas and commence expending for luxuries, until in a short time their expenses swallow up their income, and they become ruined in their ridiculous attempts to keep up appearances, and make a "sensation."

I know a gentleman of fortune who says, that when he first began to prosper, his wife would have a new and elegant sofa. "That sofa," he says, "cost me thirty thousand dollars!" When the sofa reached the house, it was found necessary to get chairs to match; then side-boards, carpets and tables "to correspond" with them, and so on through the entire stock of furniture; when at last it was found that the house itself was quite too small and old-fashioned for the furniture, and a new one was built to correspond with the new purchases; "thus," added my friend, "summing up an outlay of thirty thousand dollars, caused by that single sofa, and saddling on me, in the shape of servants, equipage, and the necessary expenses attendant upon keeping up a fine 'establishment,' a yearly outlay of eleven thousand dollars, and a tight pinch at that: whereas, ten years ago, we lived with much more real comfort, because with much less care, on as many hundreds. The truth is," he continued, "that sofa would have brought me to inevitable bankruptcy, had not a most unexampled title to prosperity kept me above it, and had I not checked the natural desire to 'cut a dash'."

The foundation of success in life is good health: that is the substratum fortune; it is also the basis of happiness. A person cannot accumulate a fortune very well when he is sick. He has no ambition; no incentive; no force. Of course, there are those who have bad health and cannot help it: you cannot expect that such persons can accumulate wealth, but there are a great many in poor health who need not be so.

Warrior Wisdom: how is your health? What aspect of your health have you not yet mastered? (Hint: it could be holding you back from wealth and freedom.)

-Mike Agugliaro

If, then, sound health is the foundation of success and happiness in life, how important it is that we should study the laws of health, which is but another expression for the laws of nature! The nearer we keep to the laws of nature, the nearer we are to good health, and yet how many persons there are who pay no attention to natural laws, but absolutely transgress them, even against their own natural inclination. We ought to know that the "sin of ignorance" is never winked at in regard to the violation of nature's laws; their infraction always brings the penalty. A child may thrust its finger into the flames without knowing it will burn, and so suffers, repentance, even, will not stop the smart. Many of our ancestors knew very little about the principle of ventilation. They did not know much about oxygen, whatever other "gin" they might have been acquainted with; and consequently they built their houses with little seven-by-nine feet bedrooms, and these good old pious Puritans would lock themselves up in one of these cells, say their prayers and go to bed. In the morning they would devoutly return thanks for the "preservation of their lives," during the night, and nobody had better reason to be thankful. Probably some big crack in the window, or in the door, let in a little fresh air, and thus saved them.

Many persons knowingly violate the laws of nature against their better impulses, for the sake of fashion. For instance, there is one thing that nothing living except a vile worm ever naturally loved, and that is tobacco; yet how many persons there are who deliberately train an unnatural appetite, and overcome this implanted aversion for tobacco, to such a degree that they get to love it. They have got hold of a poisonous, filthy weed, or rather that takes a firm hold of them. Here are married men who run about spitting tobacco juice on the carpet and floors, and sometimes even upon their wives besides. They do not kick their wives out of doors like drunken men, but their wives, I have no doubt, often wish they were outside of the house. Another perilous feature is that this artificial appetite, like jealousy, "grows by what it feeds on;" when you love that which is unnatural, a stronger appetite is created for the hurtful thing than the natural desire for what is harmless. There is an old proverb which says that "habit is second nature," but an artificial habit is stronger than nature. Take for instance, an old tobacco-chewer; his love for the "quid" is stronger than his love for any particular kind of food. He can give up roast beef easier than give up the weed.

Young lads regret that they are not men; they would like to go to bed boys and wake up men; and to accomplish this they copy the bad habits of their seniors. Little Tommy and Johnny see their fathers or uncles smoke a pipe, and they say, "If I could only do that, I would be a man too; uncle John has gone out and left his pipe of tobacco, let us try it." They take a match and light it, and then puff away. "We will learn to smoke; do you like it Johnny?" That lad dolefully replies: "Not very much; it tastes bitter;" by and by he grows pale, but he persists and he soon offers up a sacrifice on the altar of fashion; but the boys stick to it and persevere until at last they conquer their natural appetites and become the victims of acquired tastes.

Warrior Wisdom: what habits were once idle pleasures for you that have now become your master? (I'm speaking of addictions here – even seemingly innocent addictions like coffee, social media, or the praise of others.) It's very hard to spot these in your life but they are holding you back from achieving greatness.

-Mike Agugliaro

I speak "by the book," for I have noticed its effects on myself, having gone so far as to smoke ten or fifteen cigars a day; although I have not used the weed during the last fourteen years, and never shall again. The more a man smokes, the more he craves smoking; the last cigar smoked simply excites the desire for another, and so on incessantly.

Take the tobacco-chewer. In the morning, when he gets up, he puts a quid in his mouth and keeps it there all day, never taking it out except to exchange it for a fresh one, or when he is going to eat; oh! yes, at intervals during the day and evening, many a chewer takes out the quid and holds it in his hand long enough to take a drink, and then pop it goes back again. This simply proves that the appetite for rum is even stronger than that for tobacco. When the tobacco-chewer goes to your country seat and you show him your grapery and fruit house, and the beauties of your garden, when you offer him some fresh, ripe fruit, and say, "My friend, I have got here the most delicious apples, and pears, and peaches, and apricots; I have imported them from Spain, France and Italy—just see those luscious grapes; there is nothing more delicious nor more healthy than ripe fruit, so help yourself; I want to see you delight yourself with these things;" he will roll the dear quid under his tongue and answer, "No, I thank you, I have got tobacco in my mouth." His palate has become narcotized by the noxious weed, and he has lost, in a great measure, the delicate and enviable taste for fruits. This shows what expensive, useless and injurious habits men will get into. I speak from experience. I have smoked until I trembled like an aspen leaf, the blood rushed to my head, and I had a palpitation of the heart which I thought was heart disease, till I was almost killed with fright. When I consulted my physician, he said "break off tobacco using." I was not only injuring my health and spending a great deal of money, but I was setting a bad example. I obeyed his counsel. No young man in the world ever looked so beautiful, as he thought he did, behind a fifteen cent cigar or a meerschaum!

These remarks apply with tenfold force to the use of intoxicating drinks. To make money, requires a clear brain. A man has got to see that two and two make four; he must lay all his plans with reflection and forethought, and closely examine all the details and the ins and outs of business. As no man can succeed in business unless he has a brain to enable him to lay his plans, and reason to guide him in their execution, so, no matter how bountifully a man may be blessed with intelligence, if the brain is muddled, and his judgment warped by intoxicating drinks, it is impossible for him to carry on business successfully. How many good opportunities have passed, never to return, while a man was sipping a "social glass," with his friend! How many foolish bargains have been made under the influence of the "nervine," which temporarily makes its victim think he is rich. How many important chances have been put off until to-morrow, and then forever, because the wine cup has thrown the system into a state of lassitude, neutralizing the energies so essential to success in business. Verily, "wine is a mocker." The use of intoxicating drinks as a beverage, is as much an infatuation, as is the smoking of opium by the Chinese, and the former is quite as destructive to the success of the business man as the latter. It is an unmitigated evil, utterly indefensible in the light of philosophy; religion or good sense. It is the parent of nearly every other evil in our country.

Warrior Wisdom: health is a foundational requirement for wealth and freedom. If you want wealth and freedom, you MUST get healthy.

-Mike Agugliaro

Don't Mistake Your Vocation

The safest plan, and the one most sure of success for the young man starting in life, is to select the vocation which is most congenial to his tastes. Parents and guardians are often quite too negligent in regard to this. It very common for a father to say, for example: "I have five boys. I will make Billy a clergyman; John a lawyer; Tom a doctor, and Dick a farmer." He then goes into town and looks about to see what he will do with Sammy. He returns home and says "Sammy, I see watch-making is a nice genteel business; I think I will make you a goldsmith." He does this, regardless of Sam's natural inclinations, or genius.

We are all, no doubt, born for a wise purpose. There is as much diversity in our brains as in our countenances. Some are born natural mechanics, while some have great aversion to machinery. Let a dozen boys of ten years get together, and you will soon observe two or three are "whittling" out some ingenious device; working with locks or complicated machinery. When they were but five years old, their father could find no toy to please them like a puzzle. They are natural mechanics; but the other eight or nine boys have different aptitudes. I belong to the latter class; I never had the slightest love for mechanism; on the contrary, I have a sort of abhorrence for complicated machinery. I never had ingenuity enough to whittle a cider tap so it would not leak. I never could make a pen that I could write with, or understand the principle of a steam engine. If a man was to take such a boy as I was, and attempt to make a watchmaker of him, the boy might, after an apprenticeship of five or seven years, be able to take apart and put together a watch; but all through life he would be working up hill and seizing every excuse for leaving his work and idling away his time. Watchmaking is repulsive to him.

Unless a man enters upon the vocation intended for him by nature, and best suited to his peculiar genius, he cannot succeed. I am glad to believe that the majority of persons do find their right vocation. Yet we see many who have mistaken their calling, from the blacksmith up (or down) to the clergyman. You will see, for instance, that extraordinary linguist the "learned blacksmith," who ought to have been a teacher of languages; and you may have seen lawyers, doctors and clergymen who were better fitted by nature for the anvil or the lapstone.

Warrior Wisdom: take an inventory of your skills, then leverage those strengths and hire others to shore up your weaknesses.

-Mike Agugliaro

Select The Right Location

After securing the right vocation, you must be careful to select the proper location. You may have been cut out for a hotel keeper, and they say it requires a genius to "know how to keep a hotel." You might conduct a hotel like clock-work, and provide satisfactorily for five hundred guests every day; yet, if you should locate your house in a small village where there is no railroad communication or public travel, the location would be your ruin. It is equally important that you do not commence business where there are already enough to meet all demands in the same occupation.

Warrior Wisdom: businesses owners must seek out opportunities rather than operating their business wherever habit or traditional tell them.
-Mike Agugliaro

I remember a case which illustrates this subject. When I was in London in 1858, I was passing down Holborn with an English friend and came to the "penny shows." They had immense cartoons outside, portraying the wonderful curiosities to be seen "all for a penny." Being a little in the "show line" myself, I said "let us go in here." We soon found ourselves in the presence of the illustrious showman, and he proved to be the sharpest man in that line I had ever met. He told us some extraordinary stories in reference to his bearded ladies, his Albinos, and his Armadillos, which we could hardly believe, but thought it "better to believe it than look after the proof." He finally begged to call our attention to some wax statuary, and showed us a lot of the dirtiest and filthiest wax figures imaginable. They looked as if they had not seen water since the Deluge.

"What is there so wonderful about your statuary?" I asked.

"I beg you not to speak so satirically," he replied, "Sir, these are not Madam Tussaud's wax figures, all covered with gilt and tinsel and imitation diamonds, and copied from engravings and photographs. Mine, sir, were taken from life. Whenever you look upon one of those figures, you may consider that you are looking upon the living individual."

Glancing casually at them, I saw one labeled "Henry VIII," and feeling a little curious upon seeing that it looked like Calvin Edson, the living skeleton, I said: "Do you call that 'Henry the Eighth?'" He replied, "Certainly; sir; it was taken from life at Hampton Court, by special order of his majesty; on such a day."

He would have given the hour of the day if I had resisted; I said, "Everybody knows that 'Henry VIII.' was a great stout old king, and that figure is lean and lank; what do you say to that?"

"Why," he replied, "you would be lean and lank yourself if you sat there as long as he has."

There was no resisting such arguments. I said to my English friend, "Let us go out; do not tell him who I am; I show the white feather; he beats me."

He followed us to the door, and seeing the rabble in the street, he called out, "ladies and gentlemen, I beg to draw your attention to the respectable character of my visitors," pointing to us as we walked away. I called upon him a couple of days afterwards; told him who I was, and said:

"My friend, you are an excellent showman, but you have selected a bad location."

He replied, "This is true, sir; I feel that all my talents are thrown away; but what can I do?"

"You can go to America," I replied. "You can give full play to your faculties over there; you will find plenty of elbowroom in America; I will engage you for two years; after that you will be able to go on your own account."

He accepted my offer and remained two years in my New York Museum. He then went to New Orleans and carried on a traveling show business during the summer. To-day he is worth sixty thousand dollars, simply because he selected the right vocation and also secured the proper location. The old proverb says, "Three removes are as bad as a fire," but when a man is in the fire, it matters but little how soon or how often he removes.

Warrior Wisdom: shift your business to be where the opportunities are instead of wondering why there are no opportunities where your business is right now.

-Mike Agugliaro

Avoid Debt

Young men starting in life should avoid running into debt. There is scarcely anything that drags a person down like debt. It is a slavish position to get in, yet we find many a young man, hardly out of his "teens," running in debt. He meets a chum and says, "Look at this: I have got trusted for a new suit of clothes." He seems to look upon the clothes as so much given to him;

well, it frequently is so, but, if he succeeds in paying and then gets trusted again, he is adopting a habit which will keep him in poverty through life. Debt robs a man of his self-respect, and makes him almost despise himself. Grunting and groaning and working for what he has eaten up or worn out, and now when he is called upon to pay up, he has nothing to show for his money; this is properly termed "working for a dead horse." I do not speak of merchants buying and selling on credit, or of those who buy on credit in order to turn the purchase to a profit. The old Quaker said to his farmer son, "John, never get trusted; but if thee gets trusted for anything, let it be for 'manure,' because that will help thee pay it back again."

Mr. Beecher advised young men to get in debt if they could to a small amount in the purchase of land, in the country districts. "If a young man," he says, "will only get in debt for some land and then get married, these two things will keep him straight, or nothing will." This may be safe to a limited extent, but getting in debt for what you eat and drink and wear is to be avoided. Some families have a foolish habit of getting credit at "the stores," and thus frequently purchase many things which might have been dispensed with.

Warrior Wisdom: treat your debt as a tool (just as you'd treat money). Only use debt when you can build something with it.

-Mike Agugliaro

It is all very well to say; "I have got trusted for sixty days, and if I don't have the money the creditor will think nothing about it." There is no class of people in the world, who have such good memories as creditors. When the sixty days run out, you will have to pay. If you do not pay, you will break your promise, and probably resort to a falsehood. You may make some excuse or get in debt elsewhere to pay it, but that only involves you the deeper.

A good-looking, lazy young fellow, was the apprentice boy, Horatio. His employer said, "Horatio, did you ever see a snail?" "I—think—I—have," he drawled out. "You must have met him then, for I am sure you never overtook one," said the "boss." Your creditor will meet you or overtake you and say, "Now, my young friend, you agreed to pay me; you have not done it, you must give me your note." You give the note on interest and it commences working against you; "it is a dead horse." The creditor goes to bed at night and wakes up in the morning better off than when he retired to bed, because his interest has increased during the night, but you grow poorer while you are sleeping, for the interest is accumulating against you.

66

Money is in some respects like fire; it is a very excellent servant but a terrible master. When you have it mastering you; when interest is constantly piling up against you, it will keep you down in the worst kind of slavery. But let money work for you, and you have the most devoted servant in the world. It is no "eye-servant." There is nothing animate or inanimate that will work so faithfully as money when placed at interest, well secured. It works night and day, and in wet or dry weather.

I was born in the blue-law State of Connecticut, where the old Puritans had laws so rigid that it was said, "they fined a man for kissing his wife on Sunday." Yet these rich old Puritans would have thousands of dollars at interest, and on Saturday night would be worth a certain amount; on Sunday they would go to church and perform all the duties of a Christian. On waking up on Monday morning, they would find themselves considerably richer than the Saturday night previous, simply because their money placed at interest had worked faithfully for them all day Sunday, according to law!

Warrior Wisdom: your inner drive creates a business, your business creates wealth, and your wealth creates freedom. Invest in your drive, your business, and your wealth. When done correctly, these will grow even when you're not actively working in them.

-Mike Agugliaro

Do not let it work against you; if you do there is no chance for success in life so far as money is concerned. John Randolph, the eccentric Virginian, once exclaimed in Congress, "Mr. Speaker, I have discovered the philosopher's stone: pay as you go." This is, indeed, nearer to the philosopher's stone than any alchemist has ever yet arrived.

Persevere

When a man is in the right path, he must persevere. I speak of this because there are some persons who are "born tired;" naturally lazy and possessing no self-reliance and no perseverance. But they can cultivate these qualities, as Davy Crockett said:

"This thing remember, when I am dead: Be sure you are right, then go ahead."

It is this go-aheaditiveness, this determination not to let the "horrors" or the "blues" take possession of you, so as to make you relax your energies in the struggle for independence, which you must cultivate.

How many have almost reached the goal of their ambition, but, losing faith in themselves, have relaxed their energies, and the golden prize has been lost forever.

Warrior Wisdom: set targets and NEVER stop pushing toward those targets.

-Mike Agugliaro

It is, no doubt, often true, as Shakespeare says:

"There is a tide in the affairs of men, Which, taken at the flood, leads on to fortune."

If you hesitate, some bolder hand will stretch out before you and get the prize. Remember the proverb of Solomon: "He becometh poor that dealeth with a slack hand; but the hand of the diligent maketh rich."

Perseverance is sometimes but another word for self-reliance. Many persons naturally look on the dark side of life, and borrow trouble. They are born so. Then they ask for advice, and they will be governed by one wind and blown by another, and cannot rely upon themselves. Until you can get so that you can rely upon yourself, you need not expect to succeed.

I have known men, personally, who have met with pecuniary reverses, and absolutely committed suicide, because they thought they could never overcome their misfortune. But I have known others who have met more serious financial difficulties, and have bridged them over by simple perseverance, aided by a firm belief that they were doing justly, and that Providence would "overcome evil with good." You will see this illustrated in any sphere of life.

Take two generals; both understand military tactics, both educated at West Point, if you please, both equally gifted; yet one, having this principle of perseverance, and the other lacking it, the former will succeed in his profession, while the latter will fail. One may hear the cry, "the enemy are coming, and they have got cannon."

"Got cannon?" says the hesitating general.

"Yes."

"Then halt every man."

He wants time to reflect; his hesitation is his ruin; the enemy passes unmolested, or overwhelms him; while on the other hand, the general of pluck, perseverance and self-reliance, goes into battle with a will, and, amid the clash of arms, the booming of cannon, the shrieks of the wounded, and the moans of the dying, you will see this man persevering, going on, cutting and slashing his way through with unwavering determination, inspiring his soldiers to deeds of fortitude, valor, and triumph.

Warrior Wisdom: perseverance is one of two ingredients necessary for success. (The other is hard work.)

-Mike Agugliaro

Whatever You Do, Do It With All Your Might

Work at it, if necessary, early and late, in season and out of season, not leaving a stone unturned, and never deferring for a single hour that which can be done just as well now. The old proverb is full of truth and meaning, "Whatever is worth doing at all, is worth doing well." Many a man acquires a fortune by doing his business thoroughly, while his neighbor remains poor for life, because he only half does it. Ambition, energy, industry, perseverance, are indispensable requisites for success in business.

Fortune always favors the brave, and never helps a man who does not help himself. It won't do to spend your time like Mr. Micawber, in waiting for something to "turn up." To such men one of two things usually "turns up:" the poorhouse or the jail; for idleness breeds bad habits, and clothes a man in rags. The poor spendthrift vagabond says to a rich man:

"I have discovered there is enough money in the world for all of us, if it was equally divided; this must be done, and we shall all be happy together."

"But," was the response, "if everybody was like you, it would be spent in two months, and what would you do then?"

"Oh! divide again; keep dividing, of course!"

I was recently reading in a London paper an account of a like philosophic pauper who was kicked out of a cheap boarding-house because he could not pay his bill, but he had a roll of papers sticking out of his coat pocket, which, upon examination, proved to be his plan for paying off the national debt of England without the aid of a penny. People have got to do as Cromwell said: "not only trust in Providence, but keep the powder dry." Do your part of the work, or you cannot succeed. Mahomet, one night, while encamping in the desert, overheard one of his fatigued followers remark: "I will loose my camel, and trust it to God!" "No, no, not so," said the prophet, "tie thy camel, and trust it to God!" Do all you can for yourselves, and then trust to Providence, or luck, or whatever you please to call it, for the rest.

Warrior Wisdom: hard work is one of two ingredients necessary for success. (The other is perseverance.)

-Mike Agugliaro

Depend Upon Your Own Personal Exertions.

The eye of the employer is often worth more than the hands of a dozen employees. In the nature of things, an agent cannot be so faithful to his employer as to himself. Many who are employers will call to mind instances where the best employees have overlooked important points which could not have escaped their own observation as a proprietor. No man has a right to expect to succeed in life unless he understands his business, and nobody can understand his business thoroughly unless he learns it by personal application and experience. A man may be a manufacturer: he has got to learn the many details of his business personally; he will learn something every day, and he will find he will make mistakes nearly every day. And these very mistakes are helps to him in the way of experiences if he but heeds them. He will be like the Yankee tin-peddler, who, having been cheated as to quality in the purchase of his merchandise, said: "All right, there's a little information to be gained every day; I will never be cheated in that way again." Thus a man buys his experience, and it is the best kind if not purchased at too dear a rate.

Warrior Wisdom: in every experience we win — we either achieve victory or we learn in defeat.

-Mike Agugliaro

I hold that every man should, like Cuvier, the French naturalist, thoroughly know his business. So proficient was he in the study of natural history, that you might bring to him the bone, or even a section of a bone of an animal which he had never seen described, and, reasoning from analogy, he would be able to draw a picture of the object from which the bone had been taken. On one occasion his students attempted to deceive him. They rolled one of their number in a cow skin and put him under the professor's table as a new specimen. When the philosopher came into the room, some of the students asked him what animal it was. Suddenly the animal said "I am the devil and I am going to eat you." It was but natural that Cuvier should desire to classify this creature, and examining it intently, he said:

"Divided hoof; graminivorous! It cannot be done."

He knew that an animal with a split hoof must live upon grass and grain, or other kind of vegetation, and would not be inclined to eat flesh, dead or alive, so he considered himself perfectly safe. The possession of a perfect knowledge of your business is an absolute necessity in order to insure success.

Among the maxims of the elder Rothschild was one, all apparent paradox: "Be cautious and bold." This seems to be a contradiction in terms, but it is not, and there is great wisdom in the maxim. It is, in fact, a condensed statement of what I have already said. It is to say; "you must exercise your caution in laying your plans, but be bold in carrying them out." A man who is all caution, will never dare to take hold and be successful; and a man who is all boldness, is merely reckless, and must eventually fail. A man may go on "'change" and make fifty, or one hundred thousand dollars in speculating in stocks, at a single operation. But if he has simple boldness without caution, it is mere chance, and what he gains to-day he will lose to-morrow. You must have both the caution and the boldness, to insure success.

The Rothschilds have another maxim: "Never have anything to do with an unlucky man or place." That is to say, never have anything to do with a man or place which never succeeds, because, although a man may appear to be honest and intelligent, yet if he tries this or that thing and always fails, it is on account of some fault or infirmity that you may not be able to discover but nevertheless which must exist.

There is no such thing in the world as luck. There never was a man who could go out in the morning and find a purse full of gold in the street to-day, and another to-morrow, and so on, day after day: He may do so once in his life; but so far as mere luck is concerned, he is as liable to lose it as to find it. "Like causes produce like effects." If a man adopts the proper methods to be successful, "luck" will not prevent him. If he does not succeed, there are reasons for it, although, perhaps, he may not be able to see them.

 **Warrior Wisdom**: there is no such thing as luck. Chance may occasionally influence our situation but we direct our own paths. Your success is entirely dependent on you.

-Mike Agugliaro

Use The Best Tools

Men in engaging employees should be careful to get the best. Understand, you cannot have too good tools to work with, and there is no tool you should be so particular about as living tools. If you get a good one, it is better to keep him, than keep changing. He learns something every day; and you are benefited by the experience he acquires. He is worth more to you this year than last, and he is the last man to part with, provided his habits are good, and he continues faithful.

 **Warrior Wisdom**: a great team is one of the best investments you can make in your business. Pay more for the great ones, and hire too many – and your business will grow.

-Mike Agugliaro

If, as he gets more valuable, he demands an exorbitant increase of salary; on the supposition that you can't do without him, let him go. Whenever I have such an employee, I always discharge him; first, to convince him that his place may be supplied, and second, because he is good for nothing if he thinks he is invaluable and cannot be spared.

But I would keep him, if possible, in order to profit from the result of his experience. An important element in an employee is the brain. You can see bills up, "Hands Wanted," but "hands" are not worth a great deal without "heads." Mr. Beecher illustrates this, in this wise:

An employee offers his services by saving, "I have a pair of hands and one of my fingers thinks." "That is very good," says the employer. Another man comes along, and says "he has two fingers that think." "Ah! that is better." But a third calls in and says that "all his fingers and thumbs think." That is better still. Finally another steps in and says, "I have a brain that thinks; I think all over; I am a thinking as well as a working man!" "You are the man I want," says the delighted employer.

Those men who have brains and experience are therefore the most valuable and not to be readily parted with; it is better for them, as well as yourself, to keep them, at reasonable advances in their salaries from time to time.

Don't Get Above Your Business

Young men after they get through their business training, or apprenticeship, instead of pursuing their avocation and rising in their business, will often lie about doing nothing. They say; "I have learned my business, but I am not going to be a hireling; what is the object of learning my trade or profession, unless I establish myself?'"

"Have you capital to start with?"

"No, but I am going to have it."

"How are you going to get it?"

"I will tell you confidentially; I have a wealthy old aunt, and she will die pretty soon; but if she does not, I expect to find some rich old man who will lend me a few thousands to give me a start. If I only get the money to start with I will do well."

There is no greater mistake than when a young man believes he will succeed with borrowed money. Why? Because every man's experience coincides with that of Mr. Astor, who said, "it was more difficult for him to accumulate his first thousand dollars, than all the succeeding millions that made up his colossal fortune." Money is good for nothing unless you know the value of it by experience. Give a boy twenty thousand dollars and put him in business, and the chances are that he will lose every dollar of it before he is a year older. Like buying a ticket in the lottery; and drawing a prize, it is "easy come, easy go." He does not know the value of it; nothing is worth anything, unless it costs effort. Without self-denial and economy; patience and perseverance, and commencing with capital which you have not earned, you are not sure to succeed in accumulating. Young men, instead of "waiting for dead men's shoes," should be up and doing, for there is no class of persons who are so unaccommodating in regard to dying as these rich old people, and it is fortunate for the expectant heirs that it is so. Nine out of ten of the rich men of our country to-day, started out in life as poor boys, with determined wills, industry, perseverance, economy and good habits. They went on gradually, made their own money and saved it; and this is the best way to acquire a fortune. Stephen Girard started life as a poor cabin boy, and died worth nine million dollars. A.T. Stewart was a poor Irish boy; and he paid taxes on a million and a half dollars of income, per year. John Jacob Astor was a poor farmer boy, and died worth twenty millions. Cornelius Vanderbilt began life rowing a boat from Staten Island to New York; he presented our government with a steamship worth a million of dollars, and died worth fifty million. "There is no royal road to learning," says the proverb, and I may say it is equally true, "there is no royal road to wealth." But I think there is a royal road to both. The road to learning is a royal one; the road that enables the student to expand his intellect and add every day to his stock of knowledge, until, in the pleasant process of intellectual growth, he is able to solve the most profound problems, to count the stars, to analyze every atom of the globe, and to measure the firmament this is a regal highway, and it is the only road worth traveling. So in regard to wealth. Go on in confidence, study the rules, and above all things, study human nature; for "the proper study of mankind is man," and you will find that while expanding the intellect and the muscles, your enlarged experience will enable you every day to accumulate more and more principal, which will increase itself by interest and otherwise, until you arrive at a state of independence.

Warrior Wisdom: *"Go on in confidence, study the rules, and above all things, study human nature."* This is a powerful strategy of growth in your business. Apply it daily!

-Mike Agugliaro

You will find, as a general thing, that the poor boys get rich and the rich boys get poor. For instance, a rich man at his decease, leaves a large estate to his family. His eldest sons, who have helped him earn his fortune, know by experience the value of money; and they take their inheritance and add to it. The separate portions of the young children are placed at interest, and the little fellows are patted on the head, and told a dozen times a day, "you are rich; you will never have to work, you can always have whatever you wish, for you were born with a golden spoon in your mouth." The young heir soon finds out what that means; he has the finest dresses and playthings; he is crammed with sugar candies and almost "killed with kindness," and he passes from school to school, petted and flattered. He becomes arrogant and self-conceited, abuses his teachers, and carries everything with a high hand. He knows nothing of the real value of money, having never earned any; but he knows all about the "golden spoon" business. At college, he invites his poor fellow-students to his room, where he "wines and dines" them. He is cajoled and caressed, and called a glorious good follow, because he is so lavish of his money. He gives his game suppers, drives his fast horses, invites his chums to fetes and parties, determined to have lots of "good times." He spends the night in frolics and debauchery, and leads off his companions with the familiar song, "we won't go home till morning." He gets them to join him in pulling down signs, taking gates from their hinges and throwing them into back yards and horse-ponds. If the police arrest them, he knocks them down, is taken to the lockup, and joyfully foots the bills.

"Ah! my boys," he cries, "what is the use of being rich, if you can't enjoy yourself?"

He might more truly say, "if you can't make a fool of yourself;" but he is "fast," hates slow things, and doesn't "see it." Young men loaded down with other people's money are almost sure to lose all they inherit, and they acquire all sorts of bad habits which, in the majority of cases, ruin them in health, purse and character. In this country, one generation follows another, and the poor of to-day are rich in the next generation, or the third. Their experience leads them on, and they become rich, and they leave vast riches to their young children. These children, having been reared in luxury, are inexperienced and get poor; and after long experience another generation comes on and gathers up riches again in turn. And thus "history repeats itself," and happy is he who by listening to the experience of others avoids the rocks and shoals on which so many have been wrecked.

"In England, the business makes the man." If a man in that country is a mechanic or working-man, he is not recognized as a gentleman. On the occasion of my first appearance before Queen Victoria, the Duke of Wellington asked me what sphere in life General Tom Thumb's parents were in.

"His father is a carpenter," I replied.

"Oh! I had heard he was a gentleman," was the response of His Grace.

In this Republican country, the man makes the business. No matter whether he is a blacksmith, a shoemaker, a farmer, banker or lawyer, so long as his business is legitimate, he may be a gentleman. So any "legitimate" business is a double blessing it helps the man engaged in it, and also helps others. The Farmer supports his own family, but he also benefits the merchant or mechanic who needs the products of his farm. The tailor not only makes a living by his trade, but he also benefits the farmer, the clergyman and others who cannot make their own clothing. But all these classes often may be gentlemen.

The great ambition should be to excel all others engaged in the same occupation.

The college-student who was about graduating, said to an old lawyer:

"I have not yet decided which profession I will follow. Is your profession full?"

"The basement is much crowded, but there is plenty of room up-stairs," was the witty and truthful reply.

No profession, trade, or calling, is overcrowded in the upper story. Wherever you find the most honest and intelligent merchant or banker, or the best lawyer, the best doctor, the best clergyman, the best shoemaker, carpenter, or anything else, that man is most sought for, and has always enough to do. As a nation, Americans are too superficial—they are striving to get rich quickly, and do not generally do their business as substantially and thoroughly as they should, but whoever excels all others in his own line, if his habits are good and his integrity undoubted, cannot fail to secure abundant patronage, and the wealth that naturally follows. Let your motto then always be "Excelsior," for by living up to it there is no such word as fail.

Learn Something Useful

Every man should make his son or daughter learn some useful trade or profession, so that in these days of changing fortunes of being rich to-day and poor tomorrow they may have something tangible to fall back upon. This provision might save many persons from misery, who by some unexpected turn of fortune have lost all their means.

Warrior Wisdom: the home service industry is a noble trade to be in. Be proud of your contribution to making people's lives better, and do what you can to attract the next generation to the industry.

-Mike Agugliaro

Let Hope Predominate, But Be Not Too Visionary

Many persons are always kept poor, because they are too visionary. Every project looks to them like certain success, and therefore they keep changing from one business to another, always in hot water, always "under the harrow." The plan of "counting the chickens before they are hatched" is an error of ancient date, but it does not seem to improve by age.

Warrior Wisdom: plan; work the plan relentlessly; measure; adjust your course but stay focused; persevere until success. Repeat.

-Mike Agugliaro

Do Not Scatter Your Powers

Engage in one kind of business only, and stick to it faithfully until you succeed, or until your experience shows that you should abandon it. A constant hammering on one nail will generally drive it home at last, so that it can be clinched. When a man's undivided attention is centered on one object, his mind will constantly be suggesting improvements of value, which would escape him if his brain was occupied by a dozen different subjects at once. Many a fortune has slipped through a man's fingers because he was engaged in too many occupations at a time. There is good sense in the old caution against having too many irons in the fire at once.

Warrior Wisdom: a Warrior understands and uses the power of focus, while others stand back in awe of how much the Warrior achieves.

-Mike Agugliaro

Be Systematic

Men should be systematic in their business. A person who does business by rule, having a time and place for everything, doing his work promptly, will accomplish twice as much and with half the trouble of him who does it carelessly and slipshod. By introducing system into all your transactions, doing one thing at a time, always meeting appointments with punctuality, you find leisure for pastime and recreation; whereas the man who only half does one thing, and then turns to something else, and half does that, will have his business at loose ends, and will never know when his day's work is done, for it never will be done.

Warrior Wisdom: within systems and routine, there is great freedom. This seems counter-intuitive to those who are not in a routine but once you create a system and start it, you'll discover more freedom than you ever thought possible.

-Mike Agugliaro

Of course, there is a limit to all these rules. We must try to preserve the happy medium, for there is such a thing as being too systematic. There are men and women, for instance, who put away things so carefully that they can never find them again. It is too much like the "red tape" formality at Washington, and Mr. Dickens' "Circumlocution Office,"—all theory and no result.

When the "Astor House" was first started in New York City, it was undoubtedly the best hotel in the country. The proprietors had learned a good deal in Europe regarding hotels, and the landlords were proud of the rigid system which pervaded every department of their great establishment. When twelve o'clock at night had arrived, and there were a number of guests around, one of the proprietors would say, "Touch that bell, John;" and in two minutes sixty servants, with a water-bucket in each hand, would present themselves in the hall. "This," said the landlord, addressing his guests, "is our fire-bell; it will show you we are quite safe here; we do everything systematically." This was before the Croton water was introduced into the city. But they sometimes carried their system too far. On one occasion, when the hotel was thronged with guests, one of the waiters was suddenly indisposed, and although there were fifty waiters in the hotel, the landlord thought he must have his full complement, or his "system" would be interfered with. Just before dinner-time, he rushed down stairs and said, "There must be another waiter, I am one waiter short, what can I do?" He happened to see "Boots," the Irishman. "Pat," said he, "wash your hands and face; take that white apron and come into the dining-room in five minutes." Presently Pat appeared as required, and the proprietor said: "Now Pat, you must stand behind these two chairs, and wait on the gentlemen who will occupy them; did you ever act as a waiter?"

"I know all about it, sure, but I never did it."

Like the Irish pilot, on one occasion when the captain, thinking he was considerably out of his course, asked, "Are you certain you understand what you are doing?"

Pat replied, "Sure and I knows every rock in the channel."

That moment, "bang" thumped the vessel against a rock.

"Ah! be-jabers, and that is one of 'em," continued the pilot. But to return to the dining-room. "Pat," said the landlord, "here we do everything systematically. You must first give the gentlemen each a plate of soup, and when they finish that, ask them what they will have next."

Pat replied, "Ah! an' I understand parfectly the vartues of shystem."

Very soon in came the guests. The plates of soup were placed before them. One of Pat's two gentlemen ate his soup; the other did not care for it. He said: "Waiter, take this plate away and bring me some fish." Pat looked at the untasted plate of soup, and remembering the instructions of the landlord in regard to "system," replied: "Not till ye have ate yer supe!" Of course that was carrying "system" entirely too far.

Read The Newspapers

Always take a trustworthy newspaper, and thus keep thoroughly posted in regard to the transactions of the world. He who is without a newspaper is cut off from his species. In these days of telegraphs and steam, many important inventions and improvements in every branch of trade are being made, and he who don't consult the newspapers will soon find himself and his business left out in the cold.

Warrior Wisdom: don't get caught up in negative headlines. Rather, remain aware of the events and trends in the world and in your market, and seek to understand how you can benefit from them.

-Mike Agugliaro

Beware Of "Outside Operations"

We sometimes see men who have obtained fortunes, suddenly become poor. In many cases, this arises from intemperance, and often from gaming, and other bad habits. Frequently it occurs because a man has been engaged in "outside operations," of some sort. When he gets rich in his legitimate business, he is told of a grand speculation where he can make a score of thousands. He is constantly flattered by his friends, who tell him that he is born lucky, that everything he touches turns into gold. Now if he forgets that his economical habits, his rectitude of conduct and a personal attention to a business which he understood, caused his success in life, he will listen to the siren voices. He says:

"I will put in twenty thousand dollars. I have been lucky, and my good luck will soon bring me back sixty thousand dollars."

A few days elapse and it is discovered he must put in ten thousand dollars more: soon after he is told "it is all right," but certain matters not foreseen, require an advance of twenty thousand dollars more, which will bring him a rich harvest; but before the time comes around to realize, the bubble bursts, he loses all he is possessed of, and then he learns what he ought to have known at the first, that however successful a man may be in his own business, if he turns from that and engages ill a business which he don't understand, he is like Samson when shorn of his locks his strength has departed, and he becomes like other men.

If a man has plenty of money, he ought to invest something in everything that appears to promise success, and that will probably benefit mankind; but let the sums thus invested be moderate in amount, and never let a man foolishly jeopardize a fortune that he has earned in a legitimate way, by investing it in things in which he has had no experience.

Don't Endorse Without Security

I hold that no man ought ever to endorse a note or become security, for any man, be it his father or brother, to a greater extent than he can afford to lose and care nothing about, without taking good security. Here is a man that is worth twenty thousand dollars; he is doing a thriving manufacturing or mercantile trade; you are retired and living on your money; he comes to you and says:

"You are aware that I am worth twenty thousand dollars, and don't owe a dollar; if I had five thousand dollars in cash, I could purchase a particular lot of goods and double my money in a couple of months; will you endorse my note for that amount?"

You reflect that he is worth twenty thousand dollars, and you incur no risk by endorsing his note; you like to accommodate him, and you lend your name without taking the precaution of getting security. Shortly after, he shows you the note with your endorsement canceled, and tells you, probably truly, "that he made the profit that he expected by the operation," you reflect that you have done a good action, and the thought makes you feel happy. By and by, the same thing occurs again and you do it again; you have already fixed the impression in your mind that it is perfectly safe to endorse his notes without security.

But the trouble is, this man is getting money too easily. He has only to take your note to the bank, get it discounted and take the cash. He gets money for the time being without effort; without inconvenience to himself. Now mark the result. He sees a chance for speculation outside of his business. A temporary investment of only $10,000 is required. It is sure to come back before a note at the bank would be due. He places a note for that amount before you. You sign it almost mechanically. Being firmly convinced that your friend is responsible and trustworthy; you endorse his notes as a "matter of course."

Unfortunately the speculation does not come to a head quite so soon as was expected, and another $10,000 note must be discounted to take up the last one when due. Before this note matures the speculation has proved an utter failure and all the money is lost. Does the loser tell his friend, the endorser, that he has lost half of his fortune? Not at all. He don't even mention that he has speculated at all. But he has got excited; the spirit of speculation has seized him; he sees others making large sums in this way (we seldom hear of the losers), and, like other speculators, he "looks for his money where he loses it." He tries again. endorsing notes has become chronic with you, and at every loss he gets your signature for whatever amount he wants. Finally you discover your friend has lost all of his property and all of yours. You are overwhelmed with astonishment and grief, and you say "it is a hard thing; my friend here has ruined me," but, you should add, "I have also ruined him." If you had said in the first place, "I will accommodate you, but I never endorse without taking ample security," he could not have gone beyond the length of his tether, and he would never have been tempted away from his legitimate business. It is a very dangerous thing, therefore, at any time, to let people get possession of money too easily; it tempts them to hazardous speculations, if nothing more. Solomon truly said "he that hateth suretiship is sure."

So with the young man starting in business; let him understand the value of money by earning it. When he does understand its value, then grease the wheels a little in helping him to start business, but remember, men who get money with too great facility cannot usually succeed. You must get the first dollars by hard knocks, and at some sacrifice, in order to appreciate the value of those dollars.

Advertise Your Business

We all depend, more or less, upon the public for our support. We all trade with the public—lawyers, doctors, shoemakers, artists, blacksmiths, showmen, opera stagers, railroad presidents, and college professors. Those who deal with the public must be careful that their goods are valuable; that they are genuine, and will give satisfaction. When you get an article which you know is going to please your customers, and that when they have tried it, they will feel they have got their money's worth, then let the fact be known that you have got it. Be careful to advertise it in some shape or other because it is evident that if a man has ever so good an article for sale, and nobody knows it, it will bring him no return. In a country like this, where nearly everybody reads, and where newspapers are issued and circulated in editions of five thousand to two hundred thousand, it would be very unwise if this channel was not taken advantage of to reach the public in advertising. A newspaper goes into the family, and is read by wife and children, as well as the head of the home;

hence hundreds and thousands of people may read your advertisement, while you are attending to your routine business. Many, perhaps, read it while you are asleep. The whole philosophy of life is, first "sow," then "reap." That is the way the farmer does; he plants his potatoes and corn, and sows his grain, and then goes about something else, and the time comes when he reaps. But he never reaps first and sows afterwards. This principle applies to all kinds of business, and to nothing more eminently than to advertising. If a man has a genuine article, there is no way in which he can reap more advantageously than by "sowing" to the public in this way.

He must, of course, have a really good article, and one which will please his customers; anything spurious will not succeed permanently because the public is wiser than many imagine. Men and women are selfish, and we all prefer purchasing where we can get the most for our money and we try to find out where we can most surely do so.

You may advertise a spurious article, and induce many people to call and buy it once, but they will denounce you as an impostor and swindler, and your business will gradually die out and leave you poor. This is right. Few people can safely depend upon chance custom. You all need to have your customers return and purchase again. A man said to me, "I have tried advertising and did not succeed; yet I have a good article."

I replied, "My friend, there may be exceptions to a general rule. But how do you advertise?"

"I put it in a weekly newspaper three times, and paid a dollar and a half for it." I replied: "Sir, advertising is like learning—'a little is a dangerous thing!'"

A French writer says that "The reader of a newspaper does not see the first mention of an ordinary advertisement; the second insertion he sees, but does not read; the third insertion he reads; the fourth insertion, he looks at the price; the fifth insertion, he speaks of it to his wife; the sixth insertion, he is ready to purchase, and the seventh insertion, he purchases." Your object in advertising is to make the public understand what you have got to sell, and if you have not the pluck to keep advertising, until you have imparted that information, all the money you have spent is lost.

Warrior Wisdom: maximize your marketing effectiveness by increasing the frequency of your marketing exposure.

-Mike Agugliaro

You are like the fellow who told the gentleman if he would give him ten cents it would save him a dollar. "How can I help you so much with so small a sum?" asked the gentleman in surprise. "I started out this morning (hiccuped the fellow) with the full determination to get drunk, and I have spent my only dollar to accomplish the object, and it has not quite done it. Ten cents worth more of whiskey would just do it, and in this manner I should save the dollar already expended."

So a man who advertises at all must keep it up until the public know who and what he is, and what his business is, or else the money invested in advertising is lost.

Some men have a peculiar genius for writing a striking advertisement, one that will arrest the attention of the reader at first sight. This fact, of course, gives the advertiser a great advantage. Sometimes a man makes himself popular by an unique sign or a curious display in his window, recently I observed a swing sign extending over the sidewalk in front of a store, on which was the inscription in plain letters,

"Don't Read The Other Side"

Of course I did, and so did everybody else, and I learned that the man had made all independence by first attracting the public to his business in that way and then using his customers well afterwards.

Genin, the hatter, bought the first Jenny Lind ticket at auction for two hundred and twenty-five dollars, because he knew it would be a good advertisement for him. "Who is the bidder?" said the auctioneer, as he knocked down that ticket at Castle Garden. "Genin, the hatter," was the response. Here were thousands of people from the Fifth avenue, and from distant cities in the highest stations in life. "Who is 'Genin,' the hatter?" they exclaimed. They had never heard of him before. The next morning the newspapers and telegraph had circulated the facts from Maine to Texas, and from five to ten millions off people had read that the tickets sold at auction For Jenny Lind's first concert amounted to about twenty thousand dollars, and that a single ticket was sold at two hundred and twenty-five dollars, to "Genin, the hatter." Men throughout the country involuntarily took off their hats to see if they had a "Genin" hat on their heads. At a town in Iowa it was found that in the crowd around the post office, there was one man who had a "Genin" hat, and he showed it in triumph, although it was worn out and not worth two cents. "Why," one man exclaimed, "you have a real 'Genin' hat; what a lucky fellow you are." Another man said, "Hang on to that hat, it will be a valuable heir-loom in your family." Still another man in the crowd who seemed to envy the possessor of this good fortune, said, "Come, give us all a chance; put it up at auction!" He did so, and it was sold as a keepsake for nine dollars and fifty cents! What was the consequence to Mr. Genin? He sold ten thousand extra hats per annum, the first six years. Nine-tenths of the purchasers bought of him, probably, out of curiosity, and many of them, finding that he gave them an equivalent for their money, became his regular customers. This novel advertisement first struck their attention, and then, as he made a good article, they came again.

Now I don't say that everybody should advertise as Mr. Genin did. But I say if a man has got goods for sale, and he don't advertise them in some way, the chances are that some day the sheriff will do it for him. Nor do I say that everybody must advertise in a newspaper, or indeed use "printers' ink" at all. On the contrary, although that article is indispensable in the majority of cases, yet doctors and clergymen, and sometimes lawyers and some others, can more effectually reach the public in some other manner. But it is obvious, they must be known in some way, else how could they be supported?

Be Polite And Kind To Your Customers

Politeness and civility are the best capital ever invested in business. Large stores, gilt signs, flaming advertisements, will all prove unavailing if you or your employees treat your patrons abruptly. The truth is, the more kind and liberal a man is, the more generous will be the patronage bestowed upon him. "Like begets like." The man who gives the greatest amount of goods of a corresponding quality for the least sum (still reserving for himself a profit) will generally succeed best in the long run. This brings us to the golden rule, "As ye would that men should do to you, do ye also to them" and they will do better by you than if you always treated them as if you wanted to get the most you could out of them for the least return. Men who drive sharp bargains with their customers, acting as if they never expected to see them again, will not be mistaken. They will never see them again as customers. People don't like to pay and get kicked also.

One of the ushers in my Museum once told me he intended to whip a man who was in the lecture-room as soon as he came out.

"What for?" I inquired.

"Because he said I was no gentleman," replied the usher.

"Never mind," I replied, "he pays for that, and you will not convince him you are a gentleman by whipping him. I cannot afford to lose a customer. If you whip him, he will never visit the Museum again, and he will induce friends to go with him to other places of amusement instead of this, and thus you see, I should be a serious loser."

"But he insulted me," muttered the usher.

"Exactly," I replied, "and if he owned the Museum, and you had paid him for the privilege of visiting it, and he had then insulted you, there might be some reason in your resenting it, but in this instance he is the man who pays, while we receive, and you must, therefore, put up with his bad manners."

My usher laughingly remarked, that this was undoubtedly the true policy; but he added that he should not object to an increase of salary if he was expected to be abused in order to promote my interest.

 **Warrior Wisdom**: in today's world, we need to be MORE than polite and kind to customers — we need to WOW them with amazing service.

-Mike Agugliaro

Be Charitable

Of course men should be charitable, because it is a duty and a pleasure. But even as a matter of policy, if you possess no higher incentive, you will find that the liberal man will command patronage, while the sordid, uncharitable miser will be avoided.

Solomon says: "There is that scattereth and yet increaseth; and there is that withholdeth more than meet, but it tendeth to poverty." Of course the only true charity is that which is from the heart.

The best kind of charity is to help those who are willing to help themselves. Promiscuous almsgiving, without inquiring into the worthiness of the applicant, is bad in every sense. But to search out and quietly assist those who are struggling for themselves, is the kind that "scattereth and yet increaseth." But don't fall into the idea that some persons practice, of giving a prayer instead of a potato, and a benediction instead of bread, to the hungry. It is easier to make Christians with full stomachs than empty.

Don't Blab

Some men have a foolish habit of telling their business secrets. If they make money they like to tell their neighbors how it was done. Nothing is gained by this, and ofttimes much is lost. Say nothing about your profits, your hopes, your expectations, your intentions. And this should apply to letters as well as to conversation. Goethe makes Mephistophilles say: "Never write a letter nor destroy one." Business men must write letters, but they should be careful what they put in them. If you are losing money, be specially cautious and not tell of it, or you will lose your reputation.

Preserve Your Integrity

It is more precious than diamonds or rubies. The old miser said to his sons: "Get money; get it honestly if you can, but get money:" This advice was not only atrociously wicked, but it was the very essence of stupidity: It was as much as to say, "if you find it difficult to obtain money honestly, you can easily get it dishonestly. Get it in that way." Poor fool! Not to know that the most difficult thing in life is to make money dishonestly! Not to know that our prisons are full of men who attempted to follow this advice; not to understand that no man can be dishonest, without soon being found out, and that when his lack of principle is discovered, nearly every avenue to success is closed against him forever. The public very properly shun all whose integrity is doubted. No matter how polite and pleasant and accommodating a man may be, none of us dare to deal with him if we suspect "false weights and measures." Strict honesty, not only lies at the foundation of all success in life (financially), but in every other respect. Uncompromising integrity of character is invaluable. It secures to its possessor a peace and joy which cannot be attained without it—which no amount of money, or houses and lands can purchase. A man who is known to be strictly honest, may be ever so poor, but he has the purses of all the community at his disposal—for all know that if he promises to return what he borrows, he will never disappoint them. As a mere matter of selfishness, therefore, if a man had no higher motive for being honest, all will find that the maxim of Dr. Franklin can never fail to be true, that "honesty is the best policy."

To get rich, is not always equivalent to being successful. "There are many rich poor men," while there are many others, honest and devout men and women, who have never possessed so much money as some rich persons squander in a week, but who are nevertheless really richer and happier than any man can ever be while he is a transgressor of the higher laws of his being.

Warrior Wisdom: think carefully about how you define success. What does success mean to you? This definition will guide all decision-making.
                                                   -Mike Agugliaro

The inordinate love of money, no doubt, may be and is "the root of all evil," but money itself, when properly used, is not only a "handy thing to have in the house," but affords the gratification of blessing our race by enabling its possessor to enlarge the scope of human happiness and human influence. The desire for wealth is nearly universal, and none can say it is not laudable, provided the possessor of it accepts its responsibilities, and uses it as a friend to humanity.

The history of money-getting, which is commerce, is a history of civilization, and wherever trade has flourished most, there, too, have art and science produced the noblest fruits. In fact, as a general thing, money-getters are the benefactors of our race. To them, in a great measure, are we indebted for our institutions of learning and of art, our academies, colleges and churches. It is no argument against the desire for, or the possession of wealth, to say that there are sometimes misers who hoard money only for the sake of hoarding and who have no higher aspiration than to grasp everything which comes within their reach. As we have sometimes hypocrites in religion, and demagogues in politics, so there are occasionally misers among money-getters. These, however, are only exceptions to the general rule. But when, in this country, we find such a nuisance and stumbling block as a miser, we remember with gratitude that in America we have no laws of primogeniture, and that in the due course of nature the time will come when the hoarded dust will be scattered for the benefit of mankind. To all men and women, therefore, do I conscientiously say, make money honestly, and not otherwise, for Shakespeare has truly said, "He that wants money, means, and content, is without three good friends."

Applying These Timeless Secrets Today – By Mike Agugliaro

As a service business owner, part of your job is to make money. And here's the good news: there is SO MUCH opportunity to make money out there. Start by carefully analyzing how you spend your money, to ensure that your income exceeds your expenses. Track everything. Master yourself (including your health and habits) to instantly see greater success and profitability. Follow opportunities and learn from struggles. Market your business frequently to achieve growth. And remember: you are in an amazing industry. It's easy to get distracted or bogged down by the details but you help families in your market to be healthier, safer, and more comfortable!

Take Action!

___ What opportunities should you be pursuing that you're not right now?

___ What areas of your business or personal financial life need to be mastered?

_____

_____

___ What health or habit is holding you back from achieving greater success?

_____

_____

___ What needs to change in your life to work harder and persevere longer?

_____

_____

___ What systems and routines do you need to implement?

_____

_____

___ What does success mean to you? How are you doing in your pursuit of it?

_____

_____

___ Stop doing actions (Actions you currently do now but should stop doing)

_____

_____

__ Keep doing actions (Actions you currently do now and should keep doing)

_____

_____

__ Start doing actions (Actions you don't do now but should start doing)

_____

_____

__ Who will do new actions? (Assign the action to yourself or someone else)

_____

_____

__ By when? (When will these actions be complete?)

_____

_____

AN IRON WILL

Introduction By Mike Agugliaro

Orison Swett Marden lived from 1848 to 1924. He was orphaned at a young age and learned quickly the value of hard work as he worked for other families to help raise his two sisters.

A chance discovery of a book about "self help" (a new thought at the time) inspired him, and he grew up to become a successful business owner, a prolific author, and the founder of *Success Magazine*. He also earned degrees in the arts, medicine, law, and other disciplines!

Marden's first book, called *Pushing To The Front* (published in 1894), became a record-breaking best-seller of his time, and many well-known business people like Henry Ford, Thomas Edison, and J.P. Morgan consider his book an inspiration to them.

His first book was excellent but I'm going to share with you a book he wrote in 1901 called *An Iron Will*, which I think you'll gain tremendous life-changing value from.

Do you want to know the difference between success and failure? It doesn't matter whether we're talking about success or failure in business and wealth, success or failure in life and relationships, or even success or failure in something like your ability to break a habit or get out of debt. There is only one differentiating factor. It's not luck or circumstance or even knowledge or skill… it's your **will**. A successful Warrior is the one with unstoppable will.

There's a reason I've built up Gold Medal Service to $28 million a year (and growing) while other people who started businesses at the same time did not: I have the willpower to see it through. The truth is: I didn't have the willpower for a long time, which is why my business partner and I almost shut the business down after a decade of struggle. But once we decided to turn things around, I strengthened my will toward this new vision and worked relentlessly to make it happen.

There have been many books written about willpower, resolve, perseverance, and endurance (all are synonyms for will) but Marden's book was a groundbreaking, pioneering work in the concept of will, which is why I've included it here.

If you listen to me for very long – whether at one of my events or on social media or videos or my books – you'll hear this from me: I'm driven to change the lives of service business owners everywhere. Part of that vision includes helping owners discover a hidden reserve of passion and willpower within themselves for a greater life – and they leave my events or finish my books with a newfound love for their family, new inner strength to quit bad habits and start good habits, and a reborn desire to make a difference in the world.

Like the other books I've shared with you, *An Iron Will* seems dated in some ways. But the truths that lie behind the dated language are timeless, universal, and just as powerful today as they were at the beginning of the twentieth century when Marden wrote this book.

While reading, pay special attention to the following:

- What are the qualities of a strong will?
- What are the benefits of a strong will?
- How do you increase your willpower? (Hint: anyone can do it.)
- How can your past determine your future, when will is applied?
- What parts of YOUR life need to have willpower applied? (Hint: think of the bad habits and circumstances you need to end but have been avoiding, and good habits and circumstances that you desire but have not achieved yet).

Now that I've prepared you to read this book and extract its true value for your life, dive in.

Warning: This one book by Marden has the power to completely change your life by the time you finish it. If you allow it to impact you, you will be a completely different person by the end than when you began. (And that comes with another warning: if you finish the book and feel unchanged, you did not read the book as deeply as you could have).

Now here's Orison Swett Marden...

An Iron Will By Orison Swett Marden

CHAPTER I.

Training The Will.

"The education of the will is the object of our existence," says Emerson.

Nor is this putting it too strongly, if we take into account the human will in its relations to the divine. This accords with the saying of J. Stuart Mill, that "a character is a completely fashioned will."

In respect to mere mundane relations, the development and discipline of one's will-power is of supreme moment in relation to success in life. No man can ever estimate the power of will. It is a part of the divine nature, all of a piece with the power of creation. We speak of God's fiat "Fiat lux, Let light be." Man has his fiat. The achievements of history have been the choices, the determinations, the creations, of the human will. It was the will, quiet or pugnacious, gentle or grim, of men like Wilberforce and Garrison, Goodyear and Cyrus Field, Bismarck and Grant, that made them indomitable. They simply would do what they planned. Such men can no more be stopped than the sun can be, or the tide. Most men fail, not through lack of education or agreeable personal qualities, but from lack of dogged determination, from lack of dauntless will.

"It is impossible," says Sharman, "to look into the conditions under which the battle of life is being fought, without perceiving how much really depends upon the extent to which the will-power is cultivated, strengthened, and made operative in right directions." Young people need to go into training for it. We live in an age of athletic meets. Those who are determined to have athletic will-power must take for it the kind of exercise they need.

This is well illustrated by a report I have seen of the long race from Marathon in the recent Olympian games, which was won by the young Greek peasant, Sotirios Louès.

Warrior Wisdom: the mastery of your will is everything. All success and failure hinges on whether or not you can master your will.

-Mike Agugliaro

A Struggle In The Race Of Life.

There had been no great parade about the training of this champion runner. From his work at the plough he quietly betook himself to the task of making Greece victorious before the assembled strangers from every land. He was known to be a good runner, and without fuss or bustle he entered himself as a competitor. But it was not his speed alone, out-distancing every rival, that made the young Greek stand out from among his fellows that day. When he left his cottage home at Amarusi, his father said to him, "Sotiri, you must only return a victor!" The light of a firm resolve shone in the young man's eye. The old father was sure that his boy would win, and so he made his way to the station, there to wait till Sotiri should come in ahead of all the rest. No one knew the old man and his three daughters as they elbowed their way through the crowd. When at last the excitement of the assembled multitude told that the critical moment had arrived, that the racers were nearing the goal, the old father looked up through eyes that were a little dim as he realized that truly Sotiri was leading the way. He was "returning a victor." How the crowd surged about the young peasant when the race was fairly won! Wild with excitement, they knew not how to shower upon him sufficient praise. Ladies overwhelmed him with flowers and rings; some even gave him their watches, and one American lady bestowed upon him her jewelled smelling-bottle. The princes embraced him, and the king himself saluted him in military fashion. But the young Sotirios was seeking for other praise than theirs. Past the ranks of royalty and fair maidenhood, past the outstretched hands of his own countrymen, past the applauding crowd of foreigners, his gaze wandered till it fell upon an old man trembling with eagerness, who resolutely pushed his way through the excited, satisfied throng. Then the young face lighted, and as old Louès advanced to the innermost circle with arms outstretched to embrace his boy, the young victor said, simply: "You see, father, I have obeyed."

Mental Discipline.

The athlete trains for his race; and the mind must be put into training if one will win life's race.

"It is," says Professor Mathews, "only by continued, strenuous efforts, repeated again and again, day after day, week after week, and month after month, that the ability can be acquired to fasten the mind to one subject, however abstract or knotty, to the exclusion of everything else. The process of obtaining this self-mastery--this complete command of one's mental powers-- is a gradual one, its length varying with the mental constitution of each person; but its acquisition is worth infinitely more than the utmost labor it ever costs."

"Perhaps the most valuable result of all education," it was said by Professor Huxley, "is the ability to make yourself do the thing you have to do when it ought to be done, whether you like it or not; it is the first lesson which ought to be learned, and, however early a man's training begins, it is probably the last lesson which he learns thoroughly."

 **Warrior Wisdom**: Warriors willingly do what others will not. As a result, they'll reap the rewards that others will not.

-Mike Agugliaro

Doing Things Once.

When Henry Ward Beecher was asked how it was that he could accomplish so much more than other men, he replied:

"I don't do more, but less, than other people. They do all their work three times over: once in anticipation, once in actuality, once in rumination. I do mine in actuality alone, doing it once instead of three times."

This was by the intelligent exercise of Mr. Beecher's will-power in concentrating his mind upon what he was doing at a given moment, and then turning to something else. Any one who has observed business men closely, has noticed this characteristic. One of the secrets of a successful life is to be able to hold all of our energies upon one point, to focus all of the scattered rays of the mind upon one place or thing.

 **Warrior Wisdom**: your ability to concentrate on the task at hand will erase any barrier to productivity.

-Mike Agugliaro

Centralizing Force.

The mental reservoir of most people is like a leaky dam which we sometimes see in the country, where the greater part of the water flows out without going over the wheel and doing the work of the mill. The habit of mind-wandering, of worrying about this and that,

"Genius, that power which dazzles mortal eyes,
   Is oft but Perseverance in disguise."

Many a man would have been a success had he connected his fragmentary efforts. Spasmodic, disconnected attempts, without concentration, uncontrolled by any fixed idea, will never bring success. It is continuity of purpose alone that achieves results.

Learning To Swim.

The way to learn to run is to run, the way to learn to swim is to swim. The way to learn to develop will-power is by the actual exercise of will-power in the business of life. "The man that exercises his will," says an English essayist, "makes it a stronger and more effective force in proportion to the extent to which such exercise is intelligently and perseveringly maintained." The forth-putting of will-power is a means of strengthening will-power. The will becomes strong by exercise. To stick to a thing till you are master, is a test of intellectual discipline and power.

Warrior Wisdom: challenge yourself daily to increase your willpower. There is no better exercise of your mind.

-Mike Agugliaro

Dr. Cuyler.

"It is astonishing," says Dr. Theodore Cuyler, "how many men lack this power of 'holding on' until they reach the goal. They can make a sudden dash, but they lack grit. They are easily discouraged. They get on as long as everything goes smoothly, but when there is friction they lose heart. They depend on stronger personalities for their spirit and strength. They lack independence or originality. They only dare to do what others do. They do not step boldly from the crowd and act fearlessly."

The Big Trees.

What is needed by him who would succeed in the highest degree possible is careful planning. He is to accumulate reserved power, that he may be equal to all emergencies. Thomas Starr King said that the great trees of California gave him his first impression of the power of reserve. "It was the thought of the reserve energies that had been compacted into them," he said, "that stirred me. The mountains had given them their iron and rich stimulants, the hills had given them their soil, the clouds had given their rain and snow, and a thousand summers and winters had poured forth their treasures about their vast roots."

No young man can hope to do anything above the commonplace who has not made his life a reservoir of power on which he can constantly draw, which will never fail him in any emergency. Be sure that you have stored away, in your power-house, the energy, the knowledge that will be equal to the great occasion when it comes. "If I were twenty, and had but ten years to live," said a great scholar and writer, "I would spend the first nine years accumulating knowledge and getting ready for the tenth."

Warrior Wisdom: your willpower IS your power. Want more power? Get more willpower.

-Mike Agugliaro

"I Will."

"There are no two words in the English language which stand out in bolder relief, like kings upon a checker-board, to so great an extent as the words 'I will.' There is strength, depth and solidity, decision, confidence and power, determination, vigor and individuality, in the round, ringing tone which characterizes its delivery. It talks to you of triumph over difficulties, of victory in the face of discouragement, of will to promise and strength to perform, of lofty and daring enterprise, of unfettered aspirations, and of the thousand and one solid impulses by which man masters impediments in the way of progression."

Warrior Wisdom: there is strength in deciding and then acting with 100% conviction on that decision.

-Mike Agugliaro

As one has well said: "He who is silent is forgotten; he who does not advance falls back; he who stops is overwhelmed, distanced, crushed; he who ceases to become greater, becomes smaller; he who leaves off gives up; the stationary is the beginning of the end--it precedes death; to live is to achieve, to will without ceasing."

> Be thou a hero; let thy might
> Tramp on eternal snows its way,
> And through the ebon walls of night,
> Hew down a passage unto day.

Park Benjamin.

CHAPTER II.

The Rulers Of Destiny.

> There is no chance, no destiny, no fate,
> Can circumvent, or hinder, or control
> The firm resolve of a determined soul.
> Gifts count for nothing; will alone is great;
> All things give way before it soon or late.
> What obstacle can stay the mighty force
> Of the sea-seeking river in its course,
> Or cause the ascending orb of day to wait?
> Each well-born soul must win what it deserves.
> Let the fool prate of luck. The fortunate
> Is he whose earnest purpose never swerves,
> Whose slightest action or inaction serves
> The one great aim.

Ella Wheeler Wilcox.

There is always room for a man of force.--Emerson.

The king is the man who can.--Carlyle.

A strong, defiant purpose is many-handed,
and lays hold of whatever is
near that can serve it; it has a magnetic power that draws to itself
whatever is kindred.--T.T. Munger.

What is will-power, looked at in a large way, but energy of character? Energy of will, self-originating force, is the soul of every great character. Where it is, there is life; where it is not, there is faintness, helplessness, and despondency.

Warrior Wisdom: a successful person is a master of willpower. An unsuccessful person is mastered by outside forces.

-Mike Agugliaro

"Let it be your first study to teach the world that you are not wood and straw; that there is some iron in you." Men who have left their mark upon the world have been men of great and prompt decision. The achievements of will-power are almost beyond computation. Scarcely anything seems impossible to the man who can will strongly enough and long enough. One talent with a will behind it will accomplish more than ten without it, as a thimbleful of powder in a rifle, the bore of whose barrel will give it direction, will do greater execution than a carload burned in the open air.

"The Wills, The Won'ts, And The Can'ts."

"There are three kinds of people in the world," says a recent writer, "the wills, the won'ts, and the can'ts. The first accomplish everything; the second oppose everything; the third fail in everything."

Warrior Wisdom: there are three kinds of people in the world – the wills, the won't, and the can'ts. Which one are you? Which ones are on your team? Which ones are you hiring? Which ones are you training?

-Mike Agugliaro

The shores of fortune, as Foster says, are covered with the stranded wrecks of men of brilliant ability, but who have wanted courage, faith, and decision, and have therefore perished in sight of more resolute but less capable adventurers, who succeeded in making port.

Were I called upon to express in a word the secret of so many failures among those who started out with high hopes, I should say they lacked willpower. They could not half will: and what is a man without a will? He is like an engine without steam. Genius unexecuted is no more genius than a bushel of acorns is a forest of oaks.

Warrior Wisdom: it is willpower and NOT ability or intelligence or capital or even the right team that will determine your business success.

-Mike Agugliaro

Will has been called the spinal column of personality. "The will in its relation to life," says an English writer, "may be compared at once to the rudder and to the steam engine of a vessel, on the confined and related action of which it depends entirely for the direction of its course and the vigor of its movement."

Strength of will is the test of a young man's possibilities. Can he will strong enough, and hold whatever he undertakes with an iron grip? It is the iron grip that takes and holds. What chance is there in this crowding, pushing, selfish, greedy world, where everything is pusher or pushed, for a young man with no will, no grip on life? The man who would forge to the front in this competitive age must be a man of prompt and determined decision.

A Tailor's Needle.

It is in one of Ben Jonson's old plays: "When I once take the humor of a thing, I am like your tailor's needle--I go through with it."

This is not different from Richelieu, who said: "When I have once taken a resolution, I go straight to my aim; I overthrow all, I cut down all."

And in business affairs the counsel of Rothschild is to the same effect: "Do without fail that which you determine to do."

Gladstone's children were taught to accomplish to the end whatever they might begin, no matter how insignificant the undertaking might be.

Warrior Wisdom: the proof of willpower is in the results. If you are struggling in your results, you lack willpower.

-Mike Agugliaro

What Is Worse Than Rashness

It is irresolution that is worse than rashness. "He that shoots," says Feltham, "may sometimes hit the mark; but he that shoots not at all can never hit it. Irresolution is like an ague; it shakes not this nor that limb, but all the body is at once in a fit."

The man who is forever twisting and turning, backing and filling, hesitating and dawdling, shuffling and parleying, weighing and balancing, splitting hairs over non-essentials, listening to every new motive which presents itself, will never accomplish anything. But the positive man, the decided man, is a power in the world, and stands for something; you can measure him, and estimate the work that his energy will accomplish.

Opportunity is coy, is swift, is gone, before the slow, the unobservant, the indolent, or the careless can seize her. "Vigilance in watching opportunity," said Phelps, "tact and daring in seizing upon opportunity; force and persistence in crowding opportunity to its utmost of possible achievement-- these are the martial virtues which must command success." "The best men," remarked Chapin, "are not those who have waited for chances, but who have taken them; besieged the chance; conquered the chance; and made chance the servitor."

Is it not possible to classify successes and failures by their various degrees of will-power? A man who can resolve vigorously upon a course of action, and turns neither to the right nor to the left, though a paradise tempt him, who keeps his eyes upon the goal, whatever distracts him, is sure of success.

"Not every vessel that sails from Tarshish will bring back the gold of Ophir. But shall it therefore rot in the harbor? No! Give its sails to the wind!"

Conscious Power.

"Conscious power," says Mellès, "exists within the mind of every one. Sometimes its existence is unrealized, but it is there. It is there to be developed and brought forth, like the culture of that obstinate but beautiful flower, the orchid. To allow it to remain dormant is to place one's self in obscurity, to trample on one's ambition, to smother one's faculties. To develop it is to individualize all that is best within you, and give it to the world. It is by an absolute knowledge of yourself, the proper estimate of your own value."

Warrior Wisdom: willpower is conscious thought. Like a light that emits from your mind, your willpower could be faint glimmer or it can be a laser beam with the strength to cut steel.

-Mike Agugliaro

"There is hardly a reader," says an experienced educator, "who will not be able to recall the early life of at least one young man whose childhood was spent in poverty, and who, in boyhood, expressed a firm desire to secure a higher education. If, a little later, that desire became a declared resolve, soon the avenues opened to that end. That desire and resolve created an atmosphere which attracted the forces necessary to the attainment of the purpose. Many of these young men will tell us that, as long as they were hoping and striving and longing, mountains of difficulty rose before them; but that when they fashioned their hopes into fixed purposes aid came unsought to help them on the way."

Do You Believe In Yourself?

The man without self-reliance and an iron will is the plaything of chance, the puppet of his environment, the slave of circumstances. Are not doubts the greatest of enemies? If you would succeed up to the limit of your possibilities, must you not constantly hold to the belief that you are success-organized, and that you will be successful, no matter what opposes? You are never to allow a shadow of doubt to enter your mind that the Creator intended you to win in life's battle. Regard every suggestion that your life may be a failure, that you are not made like those who succeed, and that success is not for you, as a traitor, and expel it from your mind as you would a thief from your house.

There is something sublime in the youth who possesses the spirit of boldness and fearlessness, who has proper confidence in his ability to do and dare.

Warrior Wisdom: willpower starts with a strong belief in yourself and what you can offer the world.

-Mike Agugliaro

The world takes us at our own valuation. It believes in the man who believes in himself, but it has little use for the timid man, the one who is never certain of himself; who cannot rely on his own judgment, who craves advice from others, and is afraid to go ahead on his own account.

It is the man with a positive nature, the man who believes that he is equal to the emergency, who believes he can do the thing he attempts, who wins the confidence of his fellow-man. He is beloved because he is brave and self-sufficient.

Those who have accomplished great things in the world have been, as a rule, bold, aggressive, and self-confident. They dared to step out from the crowd, and act in an original way. They were not afraid to be generals.

There is little room in this crowding, competing age for the timid, vacillating youth. He who would succeed to-day must not only be brave, but must also dare to take chances. He who waits for certainty never wins.

"The law of the soul is eternal endeavor,
That bears the man onward and upward forever."

"A man can be too confiding in others, but never too confident in himself."

Never admit defeat or poverty. Stoutly assert your divine right to hold your head up and look the world in the face; step bravely to the front whatever opposes, and the world will make way for you. No one will insist upon your rights while you yourself doubt that you have any. Believe you were made for the place you fill. Put forth your whole energies. Be awake, electrify yourself; go forth to the task. A young man once said to his employer, "Don't give me an easy job. I want to handle heavy boxes, shoulder great loads. I would like to lift a big mountain and throw it into the sea,"--and he stretched out two brawny arms, while his honest eyes danced and his whole being glowed with conscious strength.

The world in its heart admires the stern, determined doer. "The world turns aside to let any man pass who knows whither he is going." "It is wonderful how even the apparent casualties of life seem to bow to a spirit that will not bow to them, and yield to assist a design, after having in vain attempted to frustrate it."

"The man who succeeds," says Prentice Mulford, "must always in mind or imagination live, move, think, and act as if he gained that success, or he never will gain it."

"We go forth," said Emerson, "austere, dedicated, believing in the iron links of Destiny, and will not turn on our heels to save our lives. A book, a bust, or only the sound of a name shoots a spark through the nerves, and we suddenly believe in will. We cannot hear of personal vigor of any kind, great power of performance, without fresh resolution."

Warrior Wisdom: replenish your willpower by reviewing your foundational "why".

-Mike Agugliaro

CHAPTER III.

Force Of Will In Camp And Field.

Oh, what miracles have been wrought by the self-confidence, the self-determination of an iron will! What impossible deeds have been performed by it! It was this that took Napoleon over the Alps in midwinter; it took Farragut and Dewey past the cannons, torpedoes, and mines of the enemy; it led Nelson and Grant to victory; it has been the great tonic in the world of discovery, invention, and art; it has helped to win the thousand triumphs in war and science which were deemed impossible.

The secret of Jeanne d'Arc's success was not alone in rare decision of character, but in the seeing of visions which inspired her to self-confidence--confidence in her divine mission.

It was an iron will that gave Nelson command of the British fleet, a title, and a statue at Trafalgar Square It was the keynote of his character when he said, "When I don't know whether to fight or not, I always fight."

It was an iron will that was brought into play when Horatius with two companions held ninety thousand Tuscans at bay until the bridge across the Tiber had been destroyed--when Leonidas at Thermopylæ checked the mighty march of Xerxes--when Themistocles off the coast of Greece shattered the Persian's Armada--when Cæsar finding his army hard pressed seized spear and buckler and snatched victory from defeat--when Winkelried gathered to his breast a sheaf of Austrian spears and opened a path for his comrades--when

Wellington fought in many climes without ever being conquered--when Ney on a hundred fields changed apparent disaster into brilliant triumph--when Sheridan arrived from Winchester as the Union retreat was becoming a route and turned the tide--when Sherman signaled his men to hold the fort knowing that their leader was coming.

History furnishes thousands of examples of men who have seized occasions to accomplish results deemed impossible by those less resolute. Prompt decision and whole-souled action sweep the world before them. Who was the organizer of the modern German empire? Was he not the man of iron?

Warrior Wisdom: think something is impossible? Apply willpower.

-Mike Agugliaro

Napoleon And Grant.

"What would you do if you were besieged in a place entirely destitute of provisions?" asked the examiner, when Napoleon was a cadet.

"If there were anything to eat in the enemy's camp, I should not be concerned."

When Paris was in the hands of a mob, and the authorities were panic-stricken, in came a man who said, "I know a young officer who can quell this mob."

"Send for him." Napoleon was sent for; he came, he subjugated the mob, he subjugated the authorities, he ruled France, then conquered Europe.

May 10, 1796, Napoleon carried the bridge at Lodi, in the face of the Austrian batteries, trained upon the French end of the structure. Behind them were six thousand troops. Napoleon massed four thousand grenadiers at the head of the bridge, with a battalion of three hundred carbineers in front. At the tap of the drum the foremost assailants wheeled from the cover of the street wall under a terrible hail of grape and canister, and attempted to pass the gateway to the bridge. The front ranks went down like stalks of grain before a reaper; the column staggered and reeled backward, and the valiant grenadiers were appalled by the task before them. Without a word or a look of reproach, Napoleon placed himself at their head, and his aids and generals rushed to his side. Forward again over heaps of dead that choked the passage, and a quick run counted by seconds only carried the column across two hundred yards of clear space, scarcely a shot from the Austrians taking effect beyond the point where the platoons wheeled for the first leap. The guns of the enemy were not aimed at the advance. The advance was too quick for the Austrian gunners. So sudden and so miraculous was it all, that the Austrian artillerists abandoned their guns instantly, and their supports fled in a panic instead of rushing to the front and meeting the French onslaught. This Napoleon had counted on in making the bold attack.

What was Napoleon but the thunderbolt of war? He once journeyed from Spain to Paris at seventeen miles an hour in the saddle.

"Is it possible to cross the path?" asked Napoleon of the engineers who had been sent to explore the dreaded pass of St. Bernard.

"Perhaps," was the hesitating reply, "it is within the limits of possibility."

"Forward, then."

Yet Ulysses S. Grant, a young man unknown to fame, with neither money nor influence, with no patrons or friends, in six years fought more battles, gained more victories, captured more prisoners, took more spoils, commanded more men, than Napoleon did in twenty years. "The great thing about him," said Lincoln, "is cool persistence."

Warrior Wisdom: willpower starts as a decision and continues as tireless persistence.

-Mike Agugliaro

"Don't Swear--Fight."

When the Spanish fire on San Juan Hill became almost unbearable, some of the Rough Riders began to swear. Colonel Wood, with the wisdom of a good leader, called out, amid the whistle of the Mauser bullets: "Don't swear--fight!"

In a skirmish at Salamanca, while the enemy's guns were pouring shot into his regiment, Sir William Napier's men became disobedient. He at once ordered a halt, and flogged four of the ringleaders under fire. The men yielded at once, and then marched three miles under a heavy cannonade as coolly as if it were a review.

When Pellisier, the Crimean chief of Zouaves, struck an officer with a whip, the man drew a pistol that missed fire. The chief replied: "Fellow, I order you a three days' arrest for not having your arms in better order."

The man of iron will is cool in the hour of danger.

"I Had To Run Like A Cyclone."

This was what Roosevelt said about his pushing on up San Juan Hill ahead of his regiment: "I had to run like a cyclone to stay in front and keep from being run over."

The personal heroism of Hobson, or of Cushing, who blew up the "Albemarle" forty years ago, was but the expression of a magnificent will power. It was this which was the basis of General Wheeler's unparalleled military advancement: a second lieutenant at twenty-three, a colonel at twenty-four, a brigadier-general at twenty-five, a major-general at twenty-six, a corps commander at twenty-seven, and a lieutenant-general at twenty-eight.

General Wheeler had sixteen horses killed under him, and a great number wounded. His saddle equipments and clothes were frequently struck by the missiles of the enemy. He was three times wounded, once painfully. He had thirty-two staff officers, or acting staff officers, killed or wounded. In almost every case they were immediately by his side. No officer was ever more exposed to the missiles of death than Joseph Wheeler.

What is this imperial characteristic of manhood, an iron will, but that which underlies all magnificent achievement, whether by heroes of the "Light Brigade" or the heroic fire-fighters of our great cities?

CHAPTER IV.

Will Power In Its Relation To Health And Disease.

I.

There is no doubt that, as a rule, great decision of character is usually accompanied by great constitutional firmness. Men who have been noted for great firmness of character have usually been strong and robust. As a rule it is the strong physical man who carries weight and conviction. Take, as an example, William the Conqueror, as he is pictured by Green in his history:

"The very spirit of the sea-robbers from whom he sprang seemed embodied in his gigantic form, his enormous strength, his savage countenance, his desperate bravery. No other knight under heaven, his enemies confessed, was William's peer. No other man could bend William's bow. His mace crashed through a ring of English warriors to the foot of the standard. He rose to his greatest heights in moments when other men despaired. No other man who ever sat upon the throne of England was this man's match."

Or, take Webster. Sydney Smith said: "Webster is a living lie; because no man on earth can be as great as he looks." Carlyle said of him: "One would incline at sight to back him against the world." His very physique was eloquent. Men yielded their wills to his at sight.

The great prizes of life ever fall to the robust, the stalwart, the strong,--not to a huge muscle or powerful frame necessarily, but to a strong vitality, a great nervous energy. It is the Lord Broughams, working almost continuously one hundred and forty-four hours; it is the Napoleons, twenty hours in the saddle; it is the Franklins, camping out in the open air at seventy; it is the Gladstones, firmly grasping the helm of the ship of state at eighty-four, tramping miles every day, and chopping down huge trees at eighty-five,--who accomplish the great things of life.

To prosper you must improve your brain power; and nothing helps the brain more than a healthy body. The race of to-day is only to be won by those who will study to keep their bodies in such good condition that their minds are able and ready to sustain that high pressure on memory and mind, which our present fierce competition engenders. It is health rather than strength that is now wanted. Health is essentially the requirement of our time to enable us to succeed in life. In all modern occupations--from the nursery to the school, from the school to the shop or world beyond--the brain and nerve strain go on, continuous, augmenting, and intensifying.

Warrior Wisdom: master your health and you'll build a foundation on which to create success.

-Mike Agugliaro

As a rule physical vigor is the condition of a great career. Stonewall Jackson, early in life, determined to conquer every weakness he had, physical, mental, and moral. He held all of his powers with a firm hand. To his great self-discipline and self-mastery he owed his success. So determined was he to harden himself to the weather that he could not be induced to wear an overcoat in winter. "I will not give in to the cold," he said. For a year, on account of dyspepsia, he lived on buttermilk and stale bread, and wore a wet shirt next his body because his doctor advised it, although everybody else ridiculed the idea. This was while he was professor at the Virginia Military Institute. His doctor advised him to retire at nine o'clock; and, no matter where he was, or who was present, he always sought his bed on the minute. He adhered rigidly through life to this stern system of discipline. Such self-training, such self-conquest, gives one great power over others. It is equal to genius itself.

Warrior Wisdom: personal discipline is a cornerstone of willpower. You cannot follow the whims of your desires and be a master of yourself.
-Mike Agugliaro

"I can do nothing," said Grant, "without nine hours' sleep."

What else is so grand as to stand on life's threshold, fresh, young, hopeful, with a consciousness of power equal to any emergency,--a master of the situation? The glory of a young man is his strength.

Our great need of the world to-day is for men and women who are good animals. To endure the strain of our concentrated civilization, the coming man and woman must have an excess of animal spirits. They must have a robustness of health. Mere absence of disease is not health. It is the overflowing fountain, not the one half full, that gives life and beauty to the valley below. Only he is healthy who exults in mere animal existence; whose very life is a luxury; who feels a bounding pulse throughout his body; who feels life in every limb, as dogs do when scouring over the field, or as boys do when gliding over fields of ice.

II.

Yet in spite of all this, in defiance of it, we know that an iron will is often triumphant in the contest with physical infirmity.

"Brave spirits are a balsam to themselves:
There is a nobleness of mind that heals
Wounds beyond salves."

"One day," said a noted rope-walker, "I signed an agreement to wheel a barrow along a rope on a given day. A day or two before I was seized with lumbago. I called in my medical man, and told him I must be cured by a certain day; not only because I should lose what I hoped to earn, but also forfeit a large sum. I got no better, and the doctor forbade my getting up. I told him, 'What do I want with your advice? If you cannot cure me, of what good is your advice?' When I got to the place, there was the doctor protesting I was unfit for the exploit. I went on, though I felt like a frog with my back. I got ready my pole and my barrow, took hold of the handles and wheeled it along the rope as well as I ever did. When I got to the end I wheeled it back again, and when this was done I was a frog again. What made me that I could wheel the barrow? It was my reserve will."

 Warrior Wisdom: when faced with setbacks, your willpower will get you through. How much willpower are you building in your life?

-Mike Agugliaro

"What does he know," asks the sage, "who has not suffered?" Did not Schiller produce his greatest tragedies in the midst of physical suffering almost amounting to torture? Handel was never greater than when, warned by palsy of the approach of death, and struggling with distress and suffering, he sat down to compose the great works which have made his name immortal in music. Beethoven was almost totally deaf and burdened with sorrow when he produced his greatest works. Milton writing "Who best can suffer, best can do," wrote at his best when in feeble health, and when poor and blind.

> "... Yet I argue not
> Against Heaven's hand or will, nor bate a jot
> Of heart or hope; but still bear up and steer
> Right onward."

The Rev. William H. Milburn, who lost his sight when a child, studied for the ministry, and was ordained before he attained his majority. He has written half a dozen books, among them a very careful history of the Mississippi Valley. He has long been chaplain of the lower house of Congress.

Blind Fanny Crosby, of New York, was a teacher of the blind for many years. She has written nearly three thousand hymns, among which are: "Pass Me not, O Gentle Saviour," "Rescue the Perishing," "Saviour More than Life to Me," and "Jesus keep Me near the Cross."

"The truest help we can render one who is afflicted," said Bishop Brooks, "is not to take his burden from him, but to call out his best energy, that he may be able to bear."

What a mighty will Darwin had! He was in continual ill health. He was in constant suffering. His patience was marvellous. No one but his wife knew what he endured. "For forty years," says his son, "he never knew one day of health;" yet during those forty years he unremittingly forced himself to do the work from which the mightiest minds and the strongest constitutions would have shrunk. He had a wonderful power of sticking to a subject. He used almost to apologize for his patience, saying that he could not bear to be beaten, as if it were a sign of weakness.

Bulwer advises us to refuse to be ill, never to tell people we are ill, never to own it ourselves. Illness is one of those things which a man should resist on principle. Do not dwell upon your ailments nor study your symptoms. Never allow yourself to be convinced that you are not complete master of yourself. Stoutly affirm your own superiority over bodily ills. We should keep a high ideal of health and harmony constantly before the mind.

Is not the mind the natural protector of the body? We cannot believe that the Creator has left the whole human race entirely at the mercy of only about half a dozen specific drugs which always act with certainty. There is a divine remedy placed within us for many of the ills we suffer. If we only knew how to use this power of will and mind to protect ourselves, many of us would be able to carry youth and cheerfulness with us into the teens of our second century. The mind has undoubted power to preserve and sustain physical youth and beauty, to keep the body strong and healthy, to renew life, and to preserve it from decay, many years longer than it does now. The longest-lived men and women have, as a rule, been those who have attained great mental and moral development. They have lived in the upper region of a higher life, beyond the reach of much of the jar, the friction, and the discords which weaken and shatter most lives.

Every physician knows that courageous people, with indomitable will, are not half as likely to contract contagious diseases as the timid, the vacillating, the irresolute. A thoughtful physician once assured a friend that if an express agent were to visit New Orleans in the yellow-fever season, having forty thousand dollars in his care, he would be in little danger of the fever so long as he kept possession of the money. Let him once deliver that into other hands, and the sooner he left the city the better.

Napoleon used to visit the plague hospitals even when the physicians dreaded to go, and actually put his hands upon the plague-stricken patients. He said the man who was not afraid could vanish the plague. A will power like this is a strong tonic to the body. Such a will has taken many men from apparent death-beds, and enabled them to perform wonderful deeds of valor. When told by his physicians that he must die, Douglas Jerrold said: "And leave a family of helpless children? I won't die." He kept his word, and lived for years.

111

Warrior Wisdom: you decide everything – your health, your wealth, your level of success, your happiness, and more. It all starts in your mind.

-Mike Agugliaro

CHAPTER V.

The Romance Of Achievement Under Difficulties.

> What doth the poor man's son inherit?
> Stout muscles, and a sinewy heart,
> A hardy frame, a hardier spirit!
> King of two hands he does his part
> In every useful toil and art:
> A heritage it seems to me,
> A king might wish to hold in fee.
>
> Lowell.

Has not God given every man a capital to start with? Are we not born rich? He is rich who has good health, a sound body, good muscles; he is rich who has a good head, a good disposition, a good heart; he is rich who has two good hands, with five chances on each. Equipped? Every man is equipped as only God could equip him. What a fortune he possesses in the marvellous mechanism of his body and mind. It is individual effort that has achieved everything worth achieving.

The Fun Of The Little Game.

A big Australian, six feet four, James Tyson, died not long since, with a property of $25,000,000, who began life as a farm hand. Tyson cared little for money. He used to say of it:

"I shall just leave it behind me when I go. I shall have done with it then, and it will not concern me afterwards. But," he would add, with a characteristic semi-exultant snap of the fingers, "the money is nothing. It was the little game that was the fun."

Being asked, "What was the little game?" he replied with an energy of concentration peculiar to him: "Fighting the desert. That has been my work. I have been fighting the desert all my life, and I have won. I have put water where was no water, and beef where was no beef. I have put fences where there were no fences, and roads where there were no roads. Nothing can undo what I have done, and millions will be happier for it after I am long dead and forgotten."

Has not self-help accomplished about all the great things of the world? How many young men falter, faint, and dally with their purpose because they have no capital to start with, and wait and wait for some good luck to give them a lift. But success is the child of drudgery and perseverance. It cannot be coaxed or bribed; pay the price, and it is yours. A constant struggle, a ceaseless battle to bring success from inhospitable surroundings, is the price of all great achievements.

Conquerors Of Fortune.

Benjamin Franklin had this tenacity of purpose in a wonderful degree. When he started in the printing business in Philadelphia, he carried his material through the streets on a wheelbarrow. He hired one room for his office, work-room, and sleeping-room. He found a formidable rival in the city and invited him to his room. Pointing to a piece of bread from which he had just eaten his dinner, he said:

"Unless you can live cheaper than I can, you cannot starve me out."

It was so that he proved the wisdom of Edmund Burke's saying, that "He that wrestles with us strengthens our nerves, and sharpens our skill: our antagonist is our helper."

Warrior Wisdom: *"our antagonist is our helper."* Those battles you fight and hardships you endure make your willpower stronger. The true Warrior with the strongest willpower seeks out hardships.
-Mike Agugliaro

113

The poor and friendless lad, George Peabody, weary, footsore, and hungry, called at a tavern in Concord, N.H., and asked to be allowed to saw wood for lodging and breakfast. Yet he put in work for everything he ever received, and out-matched the poverty of early days.

Gideon Lee could not even get shoes to wear in winter, when a boy, but he went to work barefoot in the snow. He made a bargain with himself to work sixteen hours a day. He fulfilled it to the letter, and when from interruption he lost time, he robbed himself of sleep to make it up. He became a wealthy merchant of New York, mayor of the city, and a member of Congress.

Commercial Courage.

The business affairs of a gentleman named Rouss were once in a complicated condition, owing to his conflicting interests in various states, and he was thrown into prison. While confined he wrote on the walls of his cell:

"I am forty years of age this day. When I am fifty, I shall be worth half a million; and by the time I am sixty, I shall be worth a million dollars."

He lived to accumulate more than three million dollars.

"The ruin which overtakes so many merchants," says Whipple, "is due not so much to their lack of business talent as to their lack of business nerve."

 **Warrior Wisdom**: in what aspects of your business do you lack nerve?

-Mike Agugliaro

Cyrus W. Field had retired from business with a large fortune when he became possessed with the idea that by means of a cable laid upon the bottom of the Atlantic Ocean, telegraphic communication could be established between Europe and America. He plunged into the undertaking with all the force of his being. It was an incredibly hard contest: the forests of Newfoundland, the lobby in Congress, the unskilled handling of brakes on his Agamemnon cable, a second and a third breaking of the cable at sea, the cessation of the current in a well-laid cable, the snapping of a superior cable on the Great Eastern--all these availed not to foil the iron will of Field, whose final triumph was that of mental energy in the application of science.

Four New York Journalists.

To Horace Greeley, the founder of the "Tribune," I need not allude; his story is or ought to be in every school-book.

James Brooks, once the editor and proprietor of the "Daily Express," and later an eminent congressman, began life a clerk in a store in Maine, and when twenty-one received for his pay a hogshead of New England rum. He was so eager to go to college that he started for Waterville with his trunk on his back, and when he was graduated he was so poor and plucky that he carried his trunk on his back to the station as he went home.

When James Gordon Bennett was forty years old he collected all his property, three hundred dollars, and in a cellar with a board upon two barrels for a desk, himself his own typesetter, office boy, publisher, newsboy, clerk, editor, proofreader, and printer's devil, he started the "New York Herald." He did this, after many attempts and defeats in trying to follow the routine, instead of doing his own way. Never was any man's early career a better illustration of Wendell Phillips' dictum: "What is defeat? Nothing but education; nothing but the first steps to something better."

Thurlow Weed, who was a journalist for fifty-seven years, strong, sensible, genial, tactful, and of magnificent physique, who did so much to shape public policy in the Empire State, tells a most romantic story of his boyhood:--

"I cannot ascertain how much schooling I got at Catskill, probably less than a year, certainly not a year and a half, and this was when I was not more than five or six years old. I felt a necessity, at an early age, of trying to do something for my own support.

"My first employment was in sugar-making, an occupation to which I became much attached. I now look with great pleasure upon the days and nights passed in the sap-bush. The want of shoes (which, as the snow was deep, was no small privation) was the only drawback upon my happiness. I used, however, to tie pieces of an old rag carpet around my feet, and got along pretty well, chopping wood and gathering up sap. But when the spring advanced, and bare ground appeared in spots, I threw off the old carpet encumbrance and did my work barefoot.

"There is much leisure time for boys who are making maple sugar. I devoted this time to reading, when I could obtain books; but the farmers of that period had few or no books, save their Bibles. I borrowed books whenever and wherever I could.

"I heard that a neighbor, three miles off, had borrowed from a still more distant neighbor a book of great interest. I started off, barefoot, in the snow, to obtain the treasure. There were spots of bare ground, upon which I would stop to warm my feet. And there were also, along the road, occasional lengths of log-fence from which the snow had melted, and upon which it was a luxury to walk. The book was at home, and the good people consented, upon my promise that it should be neither torn nor soiled, to lend it to me. In returning with the prize, I was too happy to think of the snow or my naked feet.

"Candles were then among the luxuries, not the necessaries, of life. If boys, instead of going to bed after dark, wanted to read, they supplied themselves with pine knots, by the light of which, in a horizontal position, they pursued their studies. In this manner, with my body in the sugar-house, and my head out of doors, where the fat pine was blazing, I read with intense interest the book I had borrowed, a 'History of the French Revolution.'"

Weed's next earning was in an iron foundry at Onondaga:

"My business was, after a casting, to temper and prepare the molding 'dogs,' myself. This was night and day work. We ate salt pork and rye and Indian bread, three times a day, and slept on straw in bunks. I liked the excitement of a furnace life."

When he went to the "Albany Argus" to learn the printing business he worked from five in the morning till nine at night.

From Humblest Beginnings.

> The more difficulties one has to encounter, within and without, the more significant and the higher in inspiration his life will be.--Horace Bushnell.

The story of Weed and of Greeley is not an uncommon one in America. Some of the most eminent men on the globe have struggled with poverty in early life and triumphed over it.

Warrior Wisdom: are you defined by your difficulties? That's a good thing… Only if they become the starting point for a new story of success that is fueled by willpower.

-Mike Agugliaro

The astronomer Kepler, whose name can never die, was kept in constant anxieties; and he told fortunes by astrology for a livelihood, saying that astrology, as the daughter of astronomy, ought to keep her mother. All sorts of service he had to accept; he made almanacs and worked for any one who would pay him.

Linnæus was so poor when getting his education that he had to mend his shoes with folded paper, and often had to beg his meals of his friends.

During the ten years in which he made his greatest discoveries, Isaac Newton could hardly pay two shillings a week to the Royal Society of which he was a member. Some of his friends wanted to get him excused from this payment, but he would not allow them to act.

Humphry Davy had but a slender chance to acquire great scientific knowledge, yet he had true mettle in him, and he made even old pans, kettles, and bottles contribute to his success, as he experimented and studied in the attic of the apothecary store where he worked.

George Stephenson was one of eight children whose parents were so poor that all lived in a single room. George had to watch cows for a neighbor, but he managed to get time to make engines of clay, with hemlock sticks for pipes. At seventeen he had charge of an engine, with his father for fireman. He could neither read nor write, but the engine was his teacher, and he a faithful student. While the other hands were playing games or loafing in liquor shops during the holidays, George was taking his machine to pieces, cleaning it, studying it, and making experiments in engines. When he had become famous as a great inventor of improvements in engines, those who had loafed and played called him lucky.

It was by steadfastly keeping at it, by indomitable will power, that these men won their positions in life.

"We rise by the things that are under our feet;
By what we have mastered of good or gain."

Talent In Tatters

Among the companions of Sir Joshua Reynolds, while he was studying his art at Rome, was a fellow-pupil of the name of Astley. They made an excursion, with some others, on a sultry day, and all except Astley took off their coats. After several taunts he was persuaded to do the same, and displayed on the back of his waistcoat a foaming waterfall. Distress had compelled him to patch his clothes with one of his own landscapes.

James Sharpies, the celebrated blacksmith artist of England, was very poor, but he often rose at three o'clock to copy books he could not buy. He would walk eighteen miles to Manchester and back after a hard day's work, to buy a shilling's worth of artist's materials. He would ask for the heaviest work in the blacksmith shop, because it took a longer time to heat at the forge, and he could thus have many spare minutes to study the precious book, which he propped up against the chimney. He was a great miser of spare moments, and used every one as though he might never see another. He devoted his leisure hours for five years to that wonderful production, "The Forge," copies of which are to be seen in many a home. It was by one unwavering aim, carried out by an iron will, that he wrought out his life triumph.

"That boy will beat me one day," said an old painter as he watched a little fellow named Michael Angelo making drawings of pot and brushes, easel and stool, and other articles in the studio. The barefoot boy did persevere until he had overcome every difficulty and become the greatest master of art the world has known. Although Michael Angelo made himself immortal in three different occupations,--and his fame might well rest upon his dome of St. Peter as an architect, upon his "Moses" as a sculptor, or upon his "Last Judgment" as a painter,--yet we find by his correspondence, now in the British Museum, that when he was at work on his colossal bronze statue of Pope Julius II., he was so poor that he could not have his younger brother come to visit him at Bologna, because he had but one bed in which he and three of his assistants slept together. Yet

> "The star of an unconquered will
> Arose in his breast,
> Serene, and resolute and still,
> And calm and self-possessed."

Concentrated Energy.

The struggles and triumphs of those who are bound to win is a never-ending tale. Nor will the procession of enthusiastic workers cease so long as the globe is turning on its axle.

Say what we will of genius, specialized in a hundred callings, yet the fact remains that no amount of genius has ever availed upon the earth unless enforced by will power to overcome the obstacles that hedge about every one who would rise above the circumstances in which he was born, or become greater than his calling. Was not Virgil the son of a porter, Horace of a shopkeeper, Demosthenes of a cutler, Milton of a money scrivener, Shakespeare of a wool stapler, and Cromwell of a brewer?

Ben Jonson, when following his trade of a mason, worked on Lincoln's Inn in London with trowel in hand and a book in his pocket. Joseph Hunter was a carpenter in youth, Robert Burns a plowman, Keats a druggist, Thomas Carlyle and Hugh Miller masons. Dante and Descartes were soldiers. Cardinal Wolsey, Defoe, and Kirke White were butchers' sons. Faraday was the son of a hostler, and his teacher, Humphry Davy, was an apprentice to an apothecary. Kepler was a waiter boy in a German hotel, Bunyan a tinker,

Copernicus the son of a Polish baker. They rose by being greater than their callings, as Arkwright rose above mere barbering, Bunyan above tinkering, Wilson above shoemaking, Lincoln above rail-splitting, and Grant above tanning. By being first-class barbers, tinkers, shoemakers, rail-splitters, tanners, they acquired the power which enabled them to become great inventors, authors, statesmen, generals. John Kay, the inventor of the fly-shuttle, James Hargreaves, who introduced the spinning-jenny, and Samuel Compton, who originated mule-spinning, were all artisans, uneducated and poor, but were endowed with natural faculties which enabled them to make a more enduring impression upon the world than anything that could have been done by the mere power of scholarship or wealth.

It cannot be said of any of these great names that their individual courses in life would have been what they were, had there been lacking a superb will power resistless as the tide to bear them upward and onward.

> Let Fortune empty her whole quiver on me,
> I have a soul that, like an ample shield,
> Can take in all, and verge enough for more;
> Fate was not mine, nor am I Fate's:
> Souls know no conquerors.

Dryden.

CHAPTER VI.

Staying Power.

> "Never give up, there are chances and changes,
> Helping the hopeful, a hundred to one;
> And, through the chaos, High Wisdom arranges
> Ever success, if you'll only hold on.
> Never give up; for the wisest is boldest,
> Knowing that Providence mingles the cup,
> And of all maxims, the best, as the oldest,
> Is the stern watchword of 'Never give up!'"

> Be firm; one constant element of luck
> Is genuine, solid, old Teutonic pluck.

Holmes.

Success in most things depends on knowing how long it takes to succeed.--Montesquieu.

The power to hold on is characteristic of all men who have accomplished anything great; they may lack in some other particular, have many weaknesses or eccentricities, but the quality of persistence is never absent from a successful man. No matter what opposition he meets or what discouragement overtakes him, drudgery cannot disgust him, obstacles cannot discourage him, labor cannot weary him; misfortune, sorrow, and reverses cannot harm him. It is not so much brilliancy of intellect, or fertility of resource, as persistency of effort, constancy of purpose, that makes a great man. Those who succeed in life are the men and women who keep everlastingly at it, who do not believe themselves geniuses, but who know that if they ever accomplish anything they must do it by determined and persistent industry.

Audubon after years of forest life had two hundred of his priceless drawings destroyed by mice.

"A poignant flame," he relates, "pierced my brain like an arrow of fire, and for several weeks I was prostrated with fever. At length physical and moral strength awoke within me. Again I took my gun, my game-bag, my portfolio, and my pencils, and plunged once more into the depths of the forests."

All are familiar with the misfortune of Carlyle while writing his "History of the French Revolution." After the first volume was ready for the press, he loaned the manuscript to a neighbor, who left it lying on the floor, and the servant girl took it to kindle the fire. It was a bitter disappointment, but Carlyle was not the man to give up. After many months of poring Over hundreds of volumes of authorities and scores of manuscripts, he reproduced that which had burned in a few minutes.

Proceed, And Light Will Dawn.

The slightest acquaintance with literary history would bring to light a multitude of heroes of poverty or misfortune, of men and women perplexed and disheartened, who have yet aroused themselves to new effort at every new obstacle.

It is related by Arago that he found under the cover of a text book he was binding a short note from D'Alembert to a student:

"Go on, sir, go on. The difficulties you meet with will resolve themselves as you advance. Proceed; and light will dawn, and shine with increasing clearness on your path."

Warrior Wisdom: the first step to succeeding with willpower is to take the first step.
-Mike Agugliaro

"That maxim," said Arago, "was my greatest master in mathematics."

Had Balzac been easily discouraged he would have hesitated at the words of warning given by his father:

"Do you know that in literature a man must be either a king or a beggar?"

"Very well," was the reply, "I will be a king."

His parents left him to his fate in a garret. For ten years he fought terrible battles with hardship and poverty, but won a great victory at last. He won it after producing forty novels that did not win.

Zola's early manhood witnessed a bitter struggle against poverty and deprivation. Until twenty he was a spoiled child; but, on his father's death, he and his mother began the battle of life in Paris. Of his dark time, Zola himself says:

"Often I went hungry for so long, that it seemed as if I must die. I scarcely tasted meat from one month's end to another, and for two days I lived on three apples. Fire, even on the coldest nights, was an undreamed-of luxury; and I was the happiest man in Paris when I could get a candle, by the light of which I might study at night."

Samuel Johnson's bare feet at Oxford showed through the holes in his shoes, yet he threw out at his window the new pair that some one left at his door. He lived for a time in London on nine cents a day. For thirteen years he had a hard struggle with want. John Locke once lived on bread and water in a Dutch garret, and Heyne slept many a night on a barn floor with only a book for his pillow. It was to poverty as a thorn urging the breast of Harriet Martineau that we owe her writings.

There are no more interesting pages in biography than those which record how Emerson, as a child, was unable to read the second volume of a certain book, because his widowed mother could not afford the amount (five cents) necessary to obtain it from the circulating library.

"Poor fellow!" said Emerson, as he looked at his delicately-reared little son, "how much he loses by not having to go through the hard experiences I had in my youth."

It was through the necessity laid upon him to earn that Emerson made his first great success in life as a teacher. "I know," he said, "no such unquestionable badge and ensign of a sovereign mind as that tenacity of purpose, which, through all change of companions or parties or fortunes, changes never, bates no jot of heart or hope, but wearies out opposition and arrives at its port."

Warrior Wisdom: a Warrior's success is forged in the furnace of difficulty.

-Mike Agugliaro

"She Can Never Succeed."

Louisa Alcott earned two hundred thousand dollars by her pen. Yet, when she was first dreaming of her power, her father handed her a manuscript one day that had been rejected by Mr. Fields, editor of the "Atlantic," with the message:

"Tell Louisa to stick to her teaching; she can never succeed as a writer."

"Tell him I will succeed as a writer, and some day I shall write for the 'Atlantic.'"

Not long after she wrote for the "Atlantic" a poem that Longfellow attributed to Emerson. And there came a time when she wrote in her diary:

"Twenty years ago I resolved to make the family independent if I could. At forty, that is done. Debts all paid, even the outlawed ones, and we have enough to be comfortable. It has cost me my health, perhaps."

"I Trample On Impossibilities":

So it was said by Lord Chatham. "Why," asked Mirabeau, "should we call ourselves men, unless it be to succeed in everything everywhere?"

"It is all very well," said Charles J. Fox, "to tell me that a young man has distinguished himself by a brilliant first speech. He may go on satisfied with his first triumph; but show me a young man who has not succeeded at first, and has then gone on, and I will back that man to do better than those who succeeded at the first trial." Cobden broke down completely the first time he appeared on a platform in Manchester, and the chairman apologized for him; but he did not give up speaking until every poor man in England had a larger, better, and cheaper loaf. Young Disraeli sprung from a hated and persecuted race, pushed his way up through the middle classes and upper classes, until he stood self-poised upon the topmost round of political and social power. At first he was scoffed at, ridiculed, rebuffed, hissed from the House of Commons; he simply said, "The time will come when you will hear me." The time did come, and he swayed the sceptre of England for a quarter of a century.

How massive was the incalculable reserve power of Lincoln as a youth; or of President Garfield, wood-chopper, bell-ringer, and sweeper-general in college!

Warrior Wisdom: what do you do when faced with impossibility?

-Mike Agugliaro

Persistent Purpose.

We hear a great deal of talk about genius, talent, luck, chance, cleverness, and fine manners playing a large part in one's success. Leaving out luck and chance, all these elements are important factors. Yet the possession of any or all of them, unaccompanied by a definite aim, a determined purpose, will not insure success. Men drift into business. They drift into society. They drift into politics. They drift into what they fondly and but vainly imagine is religion. If winds and tides are favorable, all is well; if not, all is wrong. Stalker says: "Most men merely drift through life, and the work they do is determined by a hundred different circumstances; they might as well be doing anything else, or they would prefer to be doing nothing at all." Yet whatever else may have been lacking in the giants of the race, the men who have been conspicuously successful have all had one characteristic in common--doggedness and persistence of purpose.

It does not matter how clever a youth may be, whether he leads his class in college or outshines all the other boys in his community, he will never succeed if he lacks this essential of determined persistence. Many men who might have made brilliant musicians, artists, teachers, lawyers, able physicians or surgeons, in spite of predictions to the contrary, have fallen short of success because deficient in this quality.

Persistency of purpose is a power. It creates confidence in others. Everybody believes in the determined man. When he undertakes anything his battle is half won, because not only he himself, but every one who knows him, believes that he will accomplish whatever he sets out to do. People know that it is useless to oppose a man who uses his stumbling-blocks as stepping-stones; who is not afraid of defeat; who never, in spite of calumny or criticism, shrinks from his task; who never shirks responsibility; who always keeps his compass pointed to the north star of his purpose, no matter what storms may rage about him.

Warrior Wisdom: what is your purpose? What keeps you going when others around you give up?
-Mike Agugliaro

The persistent man never stops to consider whether he is succeeding or not. The only question with him is how to push ahead, to get a little farther along, a little nearer his goal. Whether it lead over mountains, rivers, or morasses, he must reach it. Every other consideration is sacrificed to this one dominant purpose.

The success of a dull or average youth and the failure of a brilliant one is a constant surprise in American history. But if the different cases are closely analyzed we shall find that the explanation lies in the staying power of the seemingly dull boy, the ability to stand firm as a rock under all circumstances, to allow nothing to divert him from his purpose.

Three Necessary Things.

"Three things are necessary," said Charles Sumner, "first, backbone; second, backbone; third, backbone."

A good chance alone is nothing. Education is nothing without strong and vigorous resolution and stamina to make one accomplish something in the world. An encouraging start is nothing without backbone. A man who cannot stand erect, who wabbles first one way and then the other, who has no opinion of his own, or courage to think his own thought, is of very little use in this world. It is grit, it is perseverance, it is moral stamina and courage that govern the world.

At the trial of the seven bishops of the Church of England for refusing to aid the king to overthrow the Protestant faith, it was necessary to watch the officers at the doors, lest they send food to some juryman, and aid him to starve the others into an agreement. Nothing was allowed to be sent in but water for the jurymen to wash in, and they were so thirsty they drank it up. At first nine were for acquitting, and three for convicting. Two of the minority soon gave way; the third, Arnold, was obstinate. He declined to argue. Austin said to him, "Look at me. I am the largest and the strongest of the twelve; and before I will find such a petition as this libel, here will I stay till I am no bigger than a tobacco pipe." Arnold yielded at six in the morning.

Success Against Odds.

> Yes, to this thought I hold with firm persistence;
> The last result of wisdom stamps it true:
> He only earns his freedom and existence
> Who daily conquers them anew.

Goethe.

"It is interesting to notice how some minds seem almost to create themselves," says Irving, "springing up under every disadvantage, and working their solitary but irresistible way through a thousand obstacles." Opposing circumstances create strength. Opposition gives us greater power of resistance. To overcome one barrier gives us greater ability to overcome the next. History is full of examples of men and women who have redeemed themselves from disgrace, poverty, and misfortune, by the firm resolution of an iron will.

Success is not measured by what a man accomplishes, but by the opposition he has encountered, and the courage with which he has maintained the struggle against overwhelming odds. Not the distance we have run, but the obstacles we have overcome, the disadvantages under which we have made the race, will decide the prizes.

Warrior Wisdom: *"Success is not measured by what a man accomplishes, but by the opposition he has encountered, and the courage with which he has maintained the struggle against overwhelming odds."* Read that again and again until it is real in your life.

-Mike Agugliaro

"It is defeat," says Henry Ward Beecher, "that turns bone to flint, and gristle to muscle, and makes men invincible, and formed those heroic natures that are now in ascendency in the world. Do not, then, be afraid of defeat. You are never so near to victory as when defeated in a good cause."

Governor Seymour of New York, a man of great force and character, said, in reviewing his life: "If I were to wipe out twenty acts, what should they be? Should it be my business mistakes, my foolish acts (for I suppose all do foolish acts occasionally), my grievances? No; for, after all, these are the very things by which I have profited. So I finally concluded I should expunge, instead of my mistakes, my triumphs. I could not afford to dismiss the tonic of mortification, the refinement of sorrow; I needed them every one."

"Every condition, be it what it may," says Channing, "has hardships, hazards, pains. We try to escape them; we pine for a sheltered lot, for a smooth path, for cheering friends, and unbroken success. But Providence ordains storms, disasters, hostilities, sufferings; and the great question whether we shall live to any purpose or not, whether we shall grow strong in mind and heart, or be weak and pitiable, depends on nothing so much as on our use of the adverse circumstances. Outward evils are designed to school our passions, and to rouse our faculties and virtues into intenser action. Sometimes they seem to create new powers. Difficulty is the element, and resistance the true work of man. Self-culture never goes on so fast as when embarrassed circumstances, the opposition of men or the elements, unexpected changes of the times, or other forms of suffering, instead of disheartening, throw us on our inward resources, turn us for strength to God, clear up to us the great purpose of life, and inspire calm resolution. No greatness or goodness is worth much, unless tried in these fires."

> Better to stem with heart and hand
> The roaring tide of life, than lie,
> Unmindful, on its flowery strand,
> Of God's occasions drifting by!
> Better with naked nerve to bear
> The needles of this goading air,
> Than in the lap of sensual ease forego
> The godlike power to do, the godlike aim to know.
>
> Whittier.

CHAPTER VII.

The Degree Of "O.O."

When Moody first visited Ireland he was introduced by a friend to an Irish merchant who asked at once:

"Is he an O.O.?"

"Out and Out"--that was what "O.O." stood for.

"Out and Out" for God--that was what this merchant meant. He indeed is but a wooden man, and a poor stick at that, who is decided in everything else, but who never knows "where he is at" in all moral relations, being religiously nowhere.

The early books of the Hebrews have much to say about "The Valley of Decision" and the development of "Out and Out" moral character.

Wofully lacking in a well-balanced will power is the man who stands side by side with moral evil personified, in hands with it, to serve it willingly as a tool and servant.

Morally made in God's image, what is more sane, more wholesome, more fitting, for a man than his rising up promptly, decidedly, to make the Divine Will his own will in all moral action, to take it as the supreme guide to go by? It is the glory of the human will to coincide with the Divine Will. Doing this, a man's Iron Will, instead of being a malignant selfish power, will be useful in uplifting mankind.

God has spoken, or he has not spoken. If he has spoken, the wise will hear.

> We search the world for truth; we cull
> The good, the pure, the beautiful,
> From graven stone and written scroll,
> From all the flower-fields of the soul:
> And, weary seekers of the best,
> We come back laden from our quest,
> To find that all the sages said
> Is in the BOOK our mother read.

Whittier.

> O earth that blooms and birds that sing,
> O stars that shine when all is dark!
> In type and symbol thou dost bring

The Life Divine, and bid us hark,
That we may catch the chant sublime,
And, rising, pass the bounds of time;
So shall we win the goal divine,
Our immortality.

Carrol Norton.

Applying These Timeless Secrets Today – By Mike Agugliaro

An iron will – or, as I call it, "willpower" – is the greatest tool you can have in your personal toolbox. It is the one asset that will deliver more than anything else in your life. If you pursue mastery of willpower, then you become an unstoppable force, capable of achieving absolutely anything you set your mind to. Unfortunately, most people ignore willpower and allow external circumstances to dictate their lives. Not surprisingly, most people struggle and suffer, blaming anything else but themselves. If you want to be a great Warrior and achieve success in anything and everything you put your mind to then begin today to practice strengthening your willpower. Then decide on a course of action and persist tirelessly until you've achieved it.

Take Action!

__ Rate your level of willpower (high, medium, low). How can you increase it?

_____

_____

__ What areas of your life do you struggle with willpower? And, what small actions can you take right now to begin overcoming?

_____

_____

__ What actions can you take to master willpower?

_____

_____

__ What hardships do you have that you once defined as challenging, which you can now embrace as willpower-strengthening?

_____

_____

__ Stop doing actions (Actions you currently do now but should stop doing)

_____

_____

__ Keep doing actions (Actions you currently do now and should keep doing)

_____

_____

__ Start doing actions (Actions you don't do now but should start doing)

_____

_____

__ Who will do new actions? (Assign the action to yourself or someone else)

_____

_____

___ By when? (When will these actions be complete?)

_____

_____

AS A MAN THINKETH

Introduction By Mike Agugliaro

James Allen lived from 1864 to 1912. James Allen's father died when Allen was only 15 years old, forcing the young man to quit school and support his mother and siblings.

As an adult, he became a writer, first for a magazine and then he started writing his own books.

As A Man Thinketh was James Allen's third book and his most popular. At first glance, you might be puzzled by the book's point because it is loosely based on a passage from the Christian Bible, "As a man thinketh in his heart, so is he," (Proverbs 23:7 KJV). However, this was a popular form of writing of inspirational writing at the time and should not be dismissed today as being old school or overtly religious. As James Allen himself explained, *As A Man Thinketh* is really about "the power and right application of thought."

Allen's point is this: You are what you think about, you achieve what you think about, you attract what you think about. Put another way, you ascend to the level of success that you think about.

Some of you might say, "well, I think about making a ton of money in my business but I haven't achieved that yet." In response, I would point you to Allen's book because he will explain exactly what's going on: there's a difference between what you casually dream about and what you think about with every fiber of your being.

I encounter this fact when I talk to people who say they don't have time. These same people complain about not having enough time to grow their business or invest in their marriage – but they zone out for an hour or three every night in front of the television. So think of James Allen's book in this way: if you want to know what is most important to you, look at what you spend your time on. When you're at work, are you busy putting out fires and trying to keep your cool while you deal with one headache after another? And when you're at home, are you laying on the couch in front of the television, absentmindedly flipping channels? If that describes you, I know exactly what's important to you, and that is fundamentally the point of James Allen's book.

As you read about this, consider the following:

- What do you aspire to achieve in your business and your life?
- How deeply do you desire (think about) those aspirations? Most people are convinced that they really desire certain things but few truly desire anything at all except for a mediocre life.
- How are your thoughts, emotions, physiology, actions, and lifestyle all related? (Note: this is huge.)

In your service business, think about how these concepts apply to you as the owner and, more importantly, as the leader of your team. Remember this key concept: your team is looking to you to lead them, so how are you focusing your thoughts to make sure that you lead them effectively toward growth?

Are you...

... Thinking about what you want in business?

... Thinking about what your customers want?

... Thinking about what your team wants?

... Thinking about how you can help everyone get what they want?

Master this thinking and you'll be well on your way to mastering the effective use of the best strategies and tools to grow your service business.

Now get ready for some life changing insight from James Allen...

As A Man Thinketh By James Allen

The aphorism, "As a man thinketh in his heart so is he," not only embraces the whole of a man's being, but is so comprehensive as to reach out to every condition and circumstance of his life. A man is literally what he thinks, his character being the complete sum of all his thoughts.

As the plant springs from, and could not be without, the seed, so every act of a man springs from the hidden seeds of thought, and could not have appeared without them. This applies equally to those acts called "spontaneous" and "unpremeditated" as to those, which are deliberately executed.

Act is the blossom of thought, and joy and suffering are its fruits; thus does a man garner in the sweet and bitter fruitage of his own husbandry.

"Thought in the mind hath made us, What we are
By thought was wrought and built. If a man's mind
Hath evil thoughts, pain comes on him as comes
The wheel the ox behind....

..If one endure
In purity of thought, joy follows him
As his own shadow—sure."

Man is a growth by law, and not a creation by artifice, and cause and effect is as absolute and undeviating in the hidden realm of thought as in the world of visible and material things. A noble and Godlike character is not a thing of favour or chance, but is the natural result of continued effort in right thinking, the effect of long-cherished association with Godlike thoughts. An ignoble and bestial character, by the same process, is the result of the continued harbouring of grovelling thoughts.

Man is made or unmade by himself; in the armoury of thought he forges the weapons by which he destroys himself; he also fashions the tools with which he builds for himself heavenly mansions of joy and strength and peace.

 **Warrior Wisdom**: *"Man is made or unmade by himself; in the armoury of thought he forges the weapons by which he destroys himself; he also fashions the tools with which he builds for himself heavenly mansions of joy and strength and peace."* Your thoughts become your reality. Are your negative thoughts destroying you or your positive thoughts building you up?

-Mike Agugliaro

By the right choice and true application of thought, man ascends to the Divine Perfection; by the abuse and wrong application of thought, he descends below the level of the beast. Between these two extremes are all the grades of character, and man is their maker and master.

Of all the beautiful truths pertaining to the soul which have been restored and brought to light in this age, none is more gladdening or fruitful of divine promise and confidence than this—that man is the master of thought, the moulder of character, and the maker and shaper of condition, environment, and destiny.

Warrior Wisdom: you are the master of your thoughts.

-Mike Agugliaro

As a being of Power, Intelligence, and Love, and the lord of his own thoughts, man holds the key to every situation, and contains within himself that transforming and regenerative agency by which he may make himself what he wills.

Warrior Wisdom: read that paragraph again! In your thoughts, you hold the key to every situation!

-Mike Agugliaro

Man is always the master, even in his weaker and most abandoned state; but in his weakness and degradation he is the foolish master who misgoverns his "household." When he begins to reflect upon his condition, and to search diligently for the Law upon which his being is established, he then becomes the wise master, directing his energies with intelligence, and fashioning his thoughts to fruitful issues. Such is the conscious master, and man can only thus become by discovering within himself the laws of thought; which discovery is totally a matter of application, self analysis, and experience.

Only by much searching and mining, are gold and diamonds obtained, and man can find every truth connected with his being, if he will dig deep into the mine of his soul; and that he is the maker of his character, the moulder of his life, and the builder of his destiny, he may unerringly prove, if he will watch, control, and alter his thoughts, tracing their effects upon himself, upon others, and upon his life and circumstances, linking cause and effect by patient practice and investigation, and utilizing his every experience, even to the most trivial, everyday occurrence, as a means of obtaining that knowledge of himself which is Understanding, Wisdom, Power. In this direction, as in no other, is the law absolute that "He that seeketh findeth; and to him that knocketh it shall be opened;" for only by patience, practice, and ceaseless importunity can a man enter the Door of the Temple of Knowledge.

Effect Of Thought On Circumstances

Man's mind may be likened to a garden, which may be intelligently cultivated or allowed to run wild; but whether cultivated or neglected, it must, and will, bring forth. If no useful seeds are put into it, then an abundance of useless weed-seeds will fall therein, and will continue to produce their kind.

Just as a gardener cultivates his plot, keeping it free from weeds, and growing the flowers and fruits which he requires, so may a man tend the garden of his mind, weeding out all the wrong, useless, and impure thoughts, and cultivating toward perfection the flowers and fruits of right, useful, and pure thoughts. By pursuing this process, a man sooner or later discovers that he is the master-gardener of his soul, the director of his life. He also reveals, within himself, the laws of thought, and understands, with ever-increasing accuracy, how the thought-forces and mind elements operate in the shaping of his character, circumstances, and destiny.

Thought and character are one, and as character can only manifest and discover itself through environment and circumstance, the outer conditions of a person's life will always be found to be harmoniously related to his inner state. This does not mean that a man's circumstances at any given time are an indication of his entire character, but that those circumstances are so intimately connected with some vital thought-element within himself that, for the time being, they are indispensable to his development.

Warrior Wisdom: your life is a reflection of your thoughts. If you are not happy with your life, change how you think.

-Mike Agugliaro

Every man is where he is by the law of his being; the thoughts which he has built into his character have brought him there, and in the arrangement of his life there is no element of chance, but all is the result of a law which cannot err. This is just as true of those who feel "out of harmony" with their surroundings as of those who are contented with them.

As a progressive and evolving being, man is where he is that he may learn that he may grow; and as he learns the spiritual lesson which any circumstance contains for him, it passes away and gives place to other circumstances.

Man is buffeted by circumstances so long as he believes himself to be the creature of outside conditions, but when he realizes that he is a creative power, and that he may command the hidden soil and seeds of his being out of which circumstances grow, he then becomes the rightful master of himself.

That circumstances grow out of thought every man knows who has for any length of time practised self-control and self-purification, for he will have noticed that the alteration in his circumstances has been in exact ratio with his altered mental condition. So true is this that when a man earnestly applies himself to remedy the defects in his character, and makes swift and marked progress, he passes rapidly through a succession of vicissitudes.

The soul attracts that which it secretly harbours; that which it loves, and also that which it fears; it reaches the height of its cherished aspirations; it falls to the level of its unchastened desires,—and circumstances are the means by which the soul receives its own.

Every thought-seed sown or allowed to fall into the mind, and to take root there, produces its own, blossoming sooner or later into act, and bearing its own fruitage of opportunity and circumstance. Good thoughts bear good fruit, bad thoughts bad fruit.

Warrior Wisdom: every thought becomes your reality in one way or another. What thoughts are you thinking? (That answer will predict your reality in the upcoming weeks, months, and years.)
-Mike Agugliaro

The outer world of circumstance shapes itself to the inner world of thought, and both pleasant and unpleasant external conditions are factors, which make for the ultimate good of the individual. As the reaper of his own harvest, man learns both by suffering and bliss.

Following the inmost desires, aspirations, thoughts, by which he allows himself to be dominated, (pursuing the will-o'-the-wisps of impure imaginings or steadfastly walking the highway of strong and high endeavour), a man at last arrives at their fruition and fulfilment in the outer conditions of his life. The laws of growth and adjustment everywhere obtains.

A man does not come to the almshouse or the jail by the tyranny of fate or circumstance, but by the pathway of grovelling thoughts and base desires. Nor does a pure-minded man fall suddenly into crime by stress of any mere external force; the criminal thought had long been secretly fostered in the heart, and the hour of opportunity revealed its gathered power. Circumstance does not make the man; it reveals him to himself No such conditions can exist as descending into vice and its attendant sufferings apart from vicious inclinations, or ascending into virtue and its pure happiness without the continued cultivation of virtuous aspirations; and man, therefore, as the lord and master of thought, is the maker of himself the shaper and author of environment. Even at birth the soul comes to its own and through every step of its earthly pilgrimage it attracts those combinations of conditions which reveal itself, which are the reflections of its own purity and, impurity, its strength and weakness.

Men do not attract that which they want, but that which they are. Their whims, fancies, and ambitions are thwarted at every step, but their inmost thoughts and desires are fed with their own food, be it foul or clean. The "divinity that shapes our ends" is in ourselves; it is our very self. Only himself manacles man: thought and action are the jailers of Fate—they imprison, being base; they are also the angels of Freedom—they liberate, being noble. Not what he wishes and prays for does a man get, but what he justly earns. His wishes and prayers are only gratified and answered when they harmonize with his thoughts and actions.

 **Warrior Wisdom**: if you are frustrated or upset or annoyed, it's because there is misalignment between what you think should be happening and what is actually happening. The negativity will vanish when you achieve alignment.

-Mike Agugliaro

In the light of this truth, what, then, is the meaning of "fighting against circumstances?" It means that a man is continually revolting against an effect without, while all the time he is nourishing and preserving its cause in his heart. That cause may take the form of a conscious vice or an unconscious weakness; but whatever it is, it stubbornly retards the efforts of its possessor, and thus calls aloud for remedy.

Men are anxious to improve their circumstances, but are unwilling to improve themselves; they therefore remain bound. The man who does not shrink from self-crucifixion can never fail to accomplish the object upon which his heart is set. This is as true of earthly as of heavenly things. Even the man whose sole object is to acquire wealth must be prepared to make great personal sacrifices before he can accomplish his object; and how much more so he who would realize a strong and well-poised life?

 **Warrior Wisdom**: improve your thoughts to improve your life. One must always come before the other.

-Mike Agugliaro

Here is a man who is wretchedly poor. He is extremely anxious that his surroundings and home comforts should be improved, yet all the time he shirks his work, and considers he is justified in trying to deceive his employer on the ground of the insufficiency of his wages. Such a man does not understand the simplest rudiments of those principles which are the basis of true prosperity, and is not only totally unfitted to rise out of his wretchedness, but is actually attracting to himself a still deeper wretchedness by dwelling in, and acting out, indolent, deceptive, and unmanly thoughts.

Here is a rich man who is the victim of a painful and persistent disease as the result of gluttony. He is willing to give large sums of money to get rid of it, but he will not sacrifice his gluttonous desires. He wants to gratify his taste for rich and unnatural viands and have his health as well. Such a man is totally unfit to have health, because he has not yet learned the first principles of a healthy life.

Here is an employer of labour who adopts crooked measures to avoid paying the regulation wage, and, in the hope of making larger profits, reduces the wages of his workpeople. Such a man is altogether unfitted for prosperity, and when he finds himself bankrupt, both as regards reputation and riches, he blames circumstances, not knowing that he is the sole author of his condition.

I have introduced these three cases merely as illustrative of the truth that man is the causer (though nearly always is unconsciously) of his circumstances, and that, whilst aiming at a good end, he is continually frustrating its accomplishment by encouraging thoughts and desires which cannot possibly harmonize with that end. Such cases could be multiplied and varied almost indefinitely, but this is not necessary, as the reader can, if he so resolves, trace the action of the laws of thought in his own mind and life, and until this is done, mere external facts cannot serve as a ground of reasoning.

Circumstances, however, are so complicated, thought is so deeply rooted, and the conditions of happiness vary so, vastly with individuals, that a man's entire soul-condition (although it may be known to himself) cannot be judged by another from the external aspect of his life alone. A man may be honest in certain directions, yet suffer privations; a man may be dishonest in certain directions, yet acquire wealth; but the conclusion usually formed that the one man fails because of his particular honesty, and that the other prospers because of his particular dishonesty, is the result of a superficial judgment, which assumes that the dishonest man is almost totally corrupt, and the honest man almost entirely virtuous. In the light of a deeper knowledge and wider experience such judgment is found to be erroneous. The dishonest man may have some admirable virtues, which the other does, not possess; and the honest man obnoxious vices which are absent in the other. The honest man reaps the good results of his honest thoughts and acts; he also brings upon himself the sufferings, which his vices produce. The dishonest man likewise garners his own suffering and happiness.

It is pleasing to human vanity to believe that one suffers because of one's virtue; but not until a man has extirpated every sickly, bitter, and impure thought from his mind, and washed every sinful stain from his soul, can he be in a position to know and declare that his sufferings are the result of his good, and not of his bad qualities; and on the way to, yet long before he has reached, that supreme perfection, he will have found, working in his mind and life, the Great Law which is absolutely just, and which cannot, therefore, give good for evil, evil for good. Possessed of such knowledge, he will then know, looking back upon his past ignorance and blindness, that his life is, and always was, justly ordered, and that all his past experiences, good and bad, were the equitable outworking of his evolving, yet unevolved self.

Good thoughts and actions can never produce bad results; bad thoughts and actions can never produce good results. This is but saying that nothing can come from corn but corn, nothing from nettles but nettles. Men understand this law in the natural world, and work with it; but few understand it in the mental and moral world (though its operation there is just as simple and undeviating), and they, therefore, do not co-operate with it.

Suffering is always the effect of wrong thought in some direction. It is an indication that the individual is out of harmony with himself, with the Law of his being. The sole and supreme use of suffering is to purify, to burn out all that is useless and impure. Suffering ceases for him who is pure. There could be no object in burning gold after the dross had been removed, and a perfectly pure and enlightened being could not suffer.

Warrior Wisdom: what is true for yourself is also true for your team and your family. If there is negativity, anger, frustration, or bad behavior, it's because there's misalignment between inner thoughts and outer circumstances. You can serve these people by helping them find alignment.

-Mike Agugliaro

The circumstances, which a man encounters with suffering, are the result of his own mental in harmony. The circumstances, which a man encounters with blessedness, are the result of his own mental harmony. Blessedness, not material possessions, is the measure of right thought; wretchedness, not lack of material possessions, is the measure of wrong thought. A man may be cursed and rich; he may be blessed and poor. Blessedness and riches are only joined together when the riches are rightly and wisely used; and the poor man only descends into wretchedness when he regards his lot as a burden unjustly imposed.

Indigence and indulgence are the two extremes of wretchedness. They are both equally unnatural and the result of mental disorder. A man is not rightly conditioned until he is a happy, healthy, and prosperous being; and happiness, health, and prosperity are the result of a harmonious adjustment of the inner with the outer, of the man with his surroundings.

A man only begins to be a man when he ceases to whine and revile, and commences to search for the hidden justice which regulates his life. And as he adapts his mind to that regulating factor, he ceases to accuse others as the cause of his condition, and builds himself up in strong and noble thoughts; ceases to kick against circumstances, but begins to use them as aids to his more rapid progress, and as a means of discovering the hidden powers and possibilities within himself.

 **Warrior Wisdom**: since thoughts become our reality, you can master your reality by mastering your thoughts.

-Mike Agugliaro

Law, not confusion, is the dominating principle in the universe; justice, not injustice, is the soul and substance of life; and righteousness, not corruption, is the moulding and moving force in the spiritual government of the world. This being so, man has but to right himself to find that the universe is right; and during the process of putting himself right he will find that as he alters his thoughts towards things and other people, things and other people will alter towards him.

The proof of this truth is in every person, and it therefore admits of easy investigation by systematic introspection and self-analysis. Let a man radically alter his thoughts, and he will be astonished at the rapid transformation it will effect in the material conditions of his life. Men imagine that thought can be kept secret, but it cannot; it rapidly crystallizes into habit, and habit solidifies into circumstance. Bestial thoughts crystallize into habits of drunkenness and sensuality, which solidify into circumstances of destitution and disease: impure thoughts of every kind crystallize into enervating and confusing habits, which solidify into distracting and adverse circumstances: thoughts of fear, doubt, and indecision crystallize into weak, unmanly, and irresolute habits, which solidify into circumstances of failure, indigence, and slavish dependence: lazy thoughts crystallize into habits of uncleanliness and dishonesty, which solidify into circumstances of foulness and beggary: hateful and condemnatory thoughts crystallize into habits of accusation and violence, which solidify into circumstances of injury and persecution: selfish thoughts of all kinds crystallize into habits of self-seeking, which solidify into circumstances more or less distressing.

 Warrior Wisdom: indulgence and a lack of self-discipline will corrupt our thought processes and negatively alter our reality.

-Mike Agugliaro

On the other hand, beautiful thoughts of all kinds crystallize into habits of grace and kindliness, which solidify into genial and sunny circumstances: pure thoughts crystallize into habits of temperance and self-control, which solidify into circumstances of repose and peace: thoughts of courage, self-reliance, and decision crystallize into manly habits, which solidify into circumstances of success, plenty, and freedom: energetic thoughts crystallize into habits of cleanliness and industry, which solidify into circumstances of pleasantness: gentle and forgiving thoughts crystallize into habits of gentleness, which solidify into protective and preservative circumstances: loving and unselfish thoughts crystallize into habits of self-forgetfulness for others, which solidify into circumstances of sure and abiding prosperity and true riches.

A particular train of thought persisted in, be it good or bad, cannot fail to produce its results on the character and circumstances. A man cannot directly choose his circumstances, but he can choose his thoughts, and so indirectly, yet surely, shape his circumstances.

Nature helps every man to the gratification of the thoughts, which he most encourages, and opportunities are presented which will most speedily bring to the surface both the good and evil thoughts.

Let a man cease from his sinful thoughts, and all the world will soften towards him, and be ready to help him; let him put away his weakly and sickly thoughts, and lo, opportunities will spring up on every hand to aid his strong resolves; let him encourage good thoughts, and no hard fate shall bind him down to wretchedness and shame. The world is your kaleidoscope, and the varying combinations of colours, which at every succeeding moment it presents to you are the exquisitely adjusted pictures of your ever-moving thoughts.

"So You will be what you will to be;
Let failure find its false content
In that poor word, 'environment,'
But spirit scorns it, and is free.

"It masters time, it conquers space;
It cowes that boastful trickster, Chance,
And bids the tyrant Circumstance
Uncrown, and fill a servant's place.

"The human Will, that force unseen,
The offspring of a deathless Soul,
Can hew a way to any goal,
Though walls of granite intervene.

"Be not impatient in delays
But wait as one who understands;
When spirit rises and commands
The gods are ready to obey."

Effect Of Thought On Health And The Body

The body is the servant of the mind. It obeys the operations of the mind, whether they be deliberately chosen or automatically expressed. At the bidding of unlawful thoughts the body sinks rapidly into disease and decay; at the command of glad and beautiful thoughts it becomes clothed with youthfulness and beauty.

Disease and health, like circumstances, are rooted in thought. Sickly thoughts will express themselves through a sickly body. Thoughts of fear have been known to kill a man as speedily as a bullet, and they are continually killing thousands of people just as surely though less rapidly. The people who live in fear of disease are the people who get it. Anxiety quickly demoralizes the whole body, and lays it open to the entrance of disease; while impure thoughts, even if not physically indulged, will soon shatter the nervous system.

Strong, pure, and happy thoughts build up the body in vigour and grace. The body is a delicate and plastic instrument, which responds readily to the thoughts by which it is impressed, and habits of thought will produce their own effects, good or bad, upon it.

 Warrior Wisdom: thoughts become reality, even in our body. Are you thinking about your health?
-Mike Agugliaro

Men will continue to have impure and poisoned blood, so long as they propagate unclean thoughts. Out of a clean heart comes a clean life and a clean body. Out of a defiled mind proceeds a defiled life and a corrupt body. Thought is the fount of action, life, and manifestation; make the fountain pure, and all will be pure.

Change of diet will not help a man who will not change his thoughts. When a man makes his thoughts pure, he no longer desires impure food.

Clean thoughts make clean habits. The so-called saint who does not wash his body is not a saint. He who has strengthened and purified his thoughts does not need to consider the malevolent microbe.

If you would protect your body, guard your mind. If you would renew your body, beautify your mind. Thoughts of malice, envy, disappointment, despondency, rob the body of its health and grace. A sour face does not come by chance; it is made by sour thoughts. Wrinkles that mar are drawn by folly, passion, and pride.

I know a woman of ninety-six who has the bright, innocent face of a girl. I know a man well under middle age whose face is drawn into inharmonious contours. The one is the result of a sweet and sunny disposition; the other is the outcome of passion and discontent.

As you cannot have a sweet and wholesome abode unless you admit the air and sunshine freely into your rooms, so a strong body and a bright, happy, or serene countenance can only result from the free admittance into the mind of thoughts of joy and goodwill and serenity.

On the faces of the aged there are wrinkles made by sympathy, others by strong and pure thought, and others are carved by passion: who cannot distinguish them? With those who have lived righteously, age is calm, peaceful, and softly mellowed, like the setting sun. I have recently seen a philosopher on his deathbed. He was not old except in years. He died as sweetly and peacefully as he had lived.

There is no physician like cheerful thought for dissipating the ills of the body; there is no comforter to compare with goodwill for dispersing the shadows of grief and sorrow. To live continually in thoughts of ill will, cynicism, suspicion, and envy, is to be confined in a self made prison-hole. But to think well of all, to be cheerful with all, to patiently learn to find the good in all—such unselfish thoughts are the very portals of heaven; and to dwell day by day in thoughts of peace toward every creature will bring abounding peace to their possessor.

Thought And Purpose

Until thought is linked with purpose there is no intelligent accomplishment. With the majority the bark of thought is allowed to "drift" upon the ocean of life. Aimlessness is a vice, and such drifting must not continue for him who would steer clear of catastrophe and destruction.

They who have no central purpose in their life fall an easy prey to petty worries, fears, troubles, and self-pityings, all of which are indications of weakness, which lead, just as surely as deliberately planned sins (though by a different route), to failure, unhappiness, and loss, for weakness cannot persist in a power evolving universe.

Warrior Wisdom: a key indicator of thought-mastery is a clearly defined purpose. What's your purpose?

-Mike Agugliaro

A man should conceive of a legitimate purpose in his heart, and set out to accomplish it. He should make this purpose the centralizing point of his thoughts. It may take the form of a spiritual ideal, or it may be a worldly object, according to his nature at the time being; but whichever it is, he should steadily focus his thought-forces upon the object, which he has set before him. He should make this purpose his supreme duty, and should devote himself to its attainment, not allowing his thoughts to wander away into ephemeral fancies, longings, and imaginings. This is the royal road to self-control and true concentration of thought. Even if he fails again and again to accomplish his purpose (as he necessarily must until weakness is overcome), the strength of character gained will be the measure of his true success, and this will form a new starting-point for future power and triumph.

Those who are not prepared for the apprehension of a great purpose should fix the thoughts upon the faultless performance of their duty, no matter how insignificant their task may appear. Only in this way can the thoughts be gathered and focussed, and resolution and energy be developed, which being done, there is nothing which may not be accomplished.

The weakest soul, knowing its own weakness, and believing this truth that strength can only be developed by effort and practice, will, thus believing, at once begin to exert itself, and, adding effort to effort, patience to patience, and strength to strength, will never cease to develop, and will at last grow divinely strong.

As the physically weak man can make himself strong by careful and patient training, so the man of weak thoughts can make them strong by exercising himself in right thinking.

Warrior Wisdom: thought-mastery is not something you should leave up to chance. You need to practice thought mastery.

-Mike Agugliaro

To put away aimlessness and weakness, and to begin to think with purpose, is to enter the ranks of those strong ones who only recognize failure as one of the pathways to attainment; who make all conditions serve them, and who think strongly, attempt fearlessly, and accomplish masterfully.

Having conceived of his purpose, a man should mentally mark out a straight pathway to its achievement, looking neither to the right nor the left. Doubts and fears should be rigorously excluded; they are disintegrating elements, which break up the straight line of effort, rendering it crooked, ineffectual, useless. Thoughts of doubt and fear never accomplished anything, and never can. They always lead to failure. Purpose, energy, power to do, and all strong thoughts cease when doubt and fear creep in.

The will to do springs from the knowledge that we can do. Doubt and fear are the great enemies of knowledge, and he who encourages them, who does not slay them, thwarts himself at every step.

He who has conquered doubt and fear has conquered failure. His every thought is allied with power, and all difficulties are bravely met and wisely overcome. His purposes are seasonably planted, and they bloom and bring forth fruit, which does not fall prematurely to the ground.

Thought allied fearlessly to purpose becomes creative force: he who knows this is ready to become something higher and stronger than a mere bundle of wavering thoughts and fluctuating sensations; he who does this has become the conscious and intelligent wielder of his mental powers.

The Thought-Factor In Achievement

ALL that a man achieves and all that he fails to achieve is the direct result of his own thoughts. In a justly ordered universe, where loss of equipoise would mean total destruction, individual responsibility must be absolute. A man's weakness and strength, purity and impurity, are his own, and not another man's; they are brought about by himself, and not by another; and they can only be altered by himself, never by another. His condition is also his own, and not another man's. His suffering and his happiness are evolved from within. As he thinks, so he is; as he continues to think, so he remains.

A strong man cannot help a weaker unless that weaker is willing to be helped, and even then the weak man must become strong of himself; he must, by his own efforts, develop the strength which he admires in another. None but himself can alter his condition.

It has been usual for men to think and to say, "Many men are slaves because one is an oppressor; let us hate the oppressor." Now, however, there is amongst an increasing few a tendency to reverse this judgment, and to say, "One man is an oppressor because many are slaves; let us despise the slaves."

The truth is that oppressor and slave are co-operators in ignorance, and, while seeming to afflict each other, are in reality afflicting themselves. A perfect Knowledge perceives the action of law in the weakness of the oppressed and the misapplied power of the oppressor; a perfect Love, seeing the suffering, which both states entail, condemns neither; a perfect Compassion embraces both oppressor and oppressed.

Warrior Wisdom: are you a slave to your thoughts? If you have bad habits or addictions, or if you struggle with acquiring good habits, then you are a slave to your thoughts.

-Mike Agugliaro

He who has conquered weakness, and has put away all selfish thoughts, belongs neither to oppressor nor oppressed. He is free.

A man can only rise, conquer, and achieve by lifting up his thoughts. He can only remain weak, and abject, and miserable by refusing to lift up his thoughts.

Before a man can achieve anything, even in worldly things, he must lift his thoughts above slavish animal indulgence. He may not, in order to succeed, give up all animality and selfishness, by any means; but a portion of it must, at least, be sacrificed. A man whose first thought is bestial indulgence could neither think clearly nor plan methodically; he could not find and develop his latent resources, and would fail in any undertaking. Not having commenced to manfully control his thoughts, he is not in a position to control affairs and to adopt serious responsibilities. He is not fit to act independently and stand alone. But he is limited only by the thoughts, which he chooses.

There can be no progress, no achievement without sacrifice, and a man's worldly success will be in the measure that he sacrifices his confused animal thoughts, and fixes his mind on the development of his plans, and the strengthening of his resolution and self-reliance. And the higher he lifts his thoughts, the more manly, upright, and righteous he becomes, the greater will be his success, the more blessed and enduring will be his achievements.

The universe does not favour the greedy, the dishonest, the vicious, although on the mere surface it may sometimes appear to do so; it helps the honest, the magnanimous, the virtuous. All the great Teachers of the ages have declared this in varying forms, and to prove and know it a man has but to persist in making himself more and more virtuous by lifting up his thoughts.

Intellectual achievements are the result of thought consecrated to the search for knowledge, or for the beautiful and true in life and nature. Such achievements may be sometimes connected with vanity and ambition, but they are not the outcome of those characteristics; they are the natural outgrowth of long and arduous effort, and of pure and unselfish thoughts.

Spiritual achievements are the consummation of holy aspirations. He who lives constantly in the conception of noble and lofty thoughts, who dwells upon all that is pure and unselfish, will, as surely as the sun reaches its zenith and the moon its full, become wise and noble in character, and rise into a position of influence and blessedness.

Achievement, of whatever kind, is the crown of effort, the diadem of thought. By the aid of self-control, resolution, purity, righteousness, and well-directed thought a man ascends; by the aid of animality, indolence, impurity, corruption, and confusion of thought a man descends.

Warrior Wisdom: the recipe for success is simple: master your thoughts, direct them toward a target, then take massive relentless action.

-Mike Agugliaro

A man may rise to high success in the world, and even to lofty altitudes in the spiritual realm, and again descend into weakness and wretchedness by allowing arrogant, selfish, and corrupt thoughts to take possession of him.

Victories attained by right thought can only be maintained by watchfulness. Many give way when success is assured, and rapidly fall back into failure.

All achievements, whether in the business, intellectual, or spiritual world, are the result of definitely directed thought, are governed by the same law and are of the same method; the only difference lies in the object of attainment.

He who would accomplish little must sacrifice little; he who would achieve much must sacrifice much; he who would attain highly must sacrifice greatly.

Visions And Ideals

The dreamers are the saviours of the world. As the visible world is sustained by the invisible, so men, through all their trials and sins and sordid vocations, are nourished by the beautiful visions of their solitary dreamers. Humanity cannot forget its dreamers; it cannot let their ideals fade and die; it lives in them; it knows them as the realities which it shall one day see and know.

Composer, sculptor, painter, poet, prophet, sage, these are the makers of the after-world, the architects of heaven. The world is beautiful because they have lived; without them, labouring humanity would perish.

He who cherishes a beautiful vision, a lofty ideal in his heart, will one day realize it. Columbus cherished a vision of another world, and he discovered it; Copernicus fostered the vision of a multiplicity of worlds and a wider universe, and he revealed it; Buddha beheld the vision of a spiritual world of stainless beauty and perfect peace, and he entered into it.

Cherish your visions; cherish your ideals; cherish the music that stirs in your heart, the beauty that forms in your mind, the loveliness that drapes your purest thoughts, for out of them will grow all delightful conditions, all, heavenly environment; of these, if you but remain true to them, your world will at last be built.

To desire is to obtain; to aspire is to, achieve. Shall man's basest desires receive the fullest measure of gratification, and his purest aspirations starve for lack of sustenance? Such is not the Law: such a condition of things can never obtain: "ask and receive."

Dream lofty dreams, and as you dream, so shall you become. Your Vision is the promise of what you shall one day be; your Ideal is the prophecy of what you shall at last unveil.

Warrior Wisdom: since our thoughts become our reality, start thinking big, powerful thoughts!
-Mike Agugliaro

The greatest achievement was at first and for a time a dream. The oak sleeps in the acorn; the bird waits in the egg; and in the highest vision of the soul a waking angel stirs. Dreams are the seedlings of realities.

Your circumstances may be uncongenial, but they shall not long remain so if you but perceive an Ideal and strive to reach it. You cannot travel within and stand still without. Here is a youth hard pressed by poverty and labour; confined long hours in an unhealthy workshop; unschooled, and lacking all the arts of refinement. But he dreams of better things; he thinks of intelligence, of refinement, of grace and beauty. He conceives of, mentally builds up, an ideal condition of life; the vision of a wider liberty and a larger scope takes possession of him; unrest urges him to action, and he utilizes all his spare time and means, small though they are, to the development of his latent powers and resources. Very soon so altered has his mind become that the workshop can no longer hold him. It has become so out of harmony with his mentality that it falls out of his life as a garment is cast aside, and, with the growth of opportunities, which fit the scope of his expanding powers, he passes out of it forever. Years later we see this youth as a full-grown man. We find him a master of certain forces of the mind, which he wields with worldwide influence and almost unequalled power. In his hands he holds the cords of gigantic responsibilities; he speaks, and lo, lives are changed; men and women hang upon his words and remould their characters, and, sunlike, he becomes the fixed and luminous centre round which innumerable destinies revolve. He has realized the Vision of his youth. He has become one with his Ideal.

And you, too, youthful reader, will realize the Vision (not the idle wish) of your heart, be it base or beautiful, or a mixture of both, for you will always gravitate toward that which you, secretly, most love. Into your hands will be placed the exact results of your own thoughts; you will receive that which you earn; no more, no less. Whatever your present environment may be, you will fall, remain, or rise with your thoughts, your Vision, your Ideal. You will become as small as your controlling desire; as great as your dominant aspiration: in the beautiful words of Stanton Kirkham Davis, "You may be keeping accounts, and presently you shall walk out of the door that for so long has seemed to you the barrier of your ideals, and shall find yourself before an audience—the pen still behind your ear, the ink stains on your fingers and then and there shall pour out the torrent of your inspiration. You may be driving sheep, and you shall wander to the city-bucolic and open-mouthed; shall wander under the intrepid guidance of the spirit into the studio of the master, and after a time he shall say, 'I have nothing more to teach you.' And now you have become the master, who did so recently dream of great things while driving sheep. You shall lay down the saw and the plane to take upon yourself the regeneration of the world."

The thoughtless, the ignorant, and the indolent, seeing only the apparent effects of things and not the things themselves, talk of luck, of fortune, and chance. Seeing a man grow rich, they say, "How lucky he is!" Observing another become intellectual, they exclaim, "How highly favoured he is!" And noting the saintly character and wide influence of another, they remark, "How chance aids him at every turn!" They do not see the trials and failures and struggles which these men have voluntarily encountered in order to gain their experience; have no knowledge of the sacrifices they have made, of the undaunted efforts they have put forth, of the faith they have exercised, that they might overcome the apparently insurmountable, and realize the Vision of their heart. They do not know the darkness and the heartaches; they only see the light and joy, and call it "luck". They do not see the long and arduous journey, but only behold the pleasant goal, and call it "good fortune," do not understand the process, but only perceive the result, and call it chance.

In all human affairs there are efforts, and there are results, and the strength of the effort is the measure of the result. Chance is not. Gifts, powers, material, intellectual, and spiritual possessions are the fruits of effort; they are thoughts completed, objects accomplished, visions realized.

The Vision that you glorify in your mind, the Ideal that you enthrone in your heart—this you will build your life by, this you will become.

Serenity

Calmness of mind is one of the beautiful jewels of wisdom. It is the result of long and patient effort in self-control. Its presence is an indication of ripened experience, and of a more than ordinary knowledge of the laws and operations of thought.

A man becomes calm in the measure that he understands himself as a thought evolved being, for such knowledge necessitates the understanding of others as the result of thought, and as he develops a right understanding, and sees more and more clearly the internal relations of things by the action of cause and effect he ceases to fuss and fume and worry and grieve, and remains poised, steadfast, serene.

Warrior Wisdom: a Warrior is always ready for battle but always surprisingly calm.

-Mike Agugliaro

The calm man, having learned how to govern himself, knows how to adapt himself to others; and they, in turn, reverence his spiritual strength, and feel that they can learn of him and rely upon him. The more tranquil a man becomes, the greater is his success, his influence, his power for good. Even the ordinary trader will find his business prosperity increase as he develops a greater self-control and equanimity, for people will always prefer to deal with a man whose demeanour is strongly equable.

The strong, calm man is always loved and revered. He is like a shade-giving tree in a thirsty land, or a sheltering rock in a storm. "Who does not love a tranquil heart, a sweet-tempered, balanced life? It does not matter whether it rains or shines, or what changes come to those possessing these blessings, for they are always sweet, serene, and calm. That exquisite poise of character, which we call serenity is the last lesson of culture, the fruitage of the soul. It is precious as wisdom, more to be desired than gold—yea, than even fine gold. How insignificant mere money seeking looks in comparison with a serene life—a life that dwells in the ocean of Truth, beneath the waves, beyond the reach of tempests, in the Eternal Calm!

"How many people we know who sour their lives, who ruin all that is sweet and beautiful by explosive tempers, who destroy their poise of character, and make bad blood! It is a question whether the great majority of people do not ruin their lives and mar their happiness by lack of self-control. How few people we meet in life who are well balanced, who have that exquisite poise which is characteristic of the finished character!

Yes, humanity surges with uncontrolled passion, is tumultuous with ungoverned grief, is blown about by anxiety and doubt only the wise man, only he whose thoughts are controlled and purified, makes the winds and the storms of the soul obey him.

Tempest-tossed souls, wherever ye may be, under whatsoever conditions ye may live, know this in the ocean of life the isles of Blessedness are smiling, and the sunny shore of your ideal awaits your coming. Keep your hand firmly upon the helm of thought. In the bark of your soul reclines the commanding Master; He does but sleep: wake Him. Self-control is strength; Right Thought is mastery; Calmness is power. Say unto your heart, "Peace, be still!"

Applying These Timeless Secrets Today – By Mike Agugliaro

People tend to separate their reality into two spheres – what goes on inside their head and what happens externally. Often, it's perceived that our thoughts are passive reflections while the external forces influence us. However, it's the opposite that is true: our thoughts create our reality. Most people think little, negative thoughts – and they lead little, negative lives. But the Warrior realizes that thoughts are powerful reality-shapers so the Warrior thinks big, thrilling thoughts and watches while life conforms to those thoughts. If you ever feel frustration or discord, it's because there is a disconnect between your thoughts and your reality and you will continue to feel that negativity until your thoughts and your reality align. If you want to succeed at anything in life, start mastering your thoughts and start thinking like a Warrior.

Take Action!

___ What kind of thoughts do you think? (Small? Negative? Depressing? Big? Positive? Exciting?) How can you stop the negative thoughts while encouraging the positive thoughts?

_____

_____

___ In what areas of your life are you currently dissatisfied or unhappy? What is the misalignment between your thought and your reality?

_____

_____

_____

___ How can you master your thoughts?

_____

_____

__ How can you improve your thoughts?

_____

_____

__ List some areas where you are thinking too small.

_____

_____

_____

__ Stop doing actions (Actions you currently do now but should stop doing)

_____

_____

__ Keep doing actions (Actions you currently do now and should keep doing)

_____

_____

__ Start doing actions (Actions you don't do now but should start doing)

_____

_____

__ Who will do new actions? (Assign the action to yourself or someone else)

_____

_____

___ By when? (When will these actions be complete?)

_____

_____

SUMMARY OF WARRIOR WISDOM

In this section of the book, I've gathered together all of the Warrior Wisdom from throughout the book. There is value to making notes in the places that these originally appeared in the book (since there is some context and other lessons around them) but I'm providing these lessons here as an additional resource and reminder for you.

Warrior Wisdom From *Acres Of Diamonds*

- There is so much power in listening – even to those we might not immediately realize have lessons to teach us.

- In every business, in every market, there are "acres of diamonds." I see them all the time (even in the markets of those who claim that they're all "mined out"). In nearly every service business, the overlooked acres of diamonds include: people, growth, profit, added services, and so much more.

- Sometimes our own knowledge, assumptions, and limiting beliefs get in our way and keep us from seeing the true riches that exist right before our eyes.

- There is value to head knowledge but only if it serves you. Always learn, but be the master of your own knowledge; don't let it master you.

- What are the acres of diamonds in your business and your market? Before you answer "none at all," consider the lessons that you've just read and spend some time giving some serious thought to your answer.

- "The opportunity to get rich, to attain unto great wealth, is here in Philadelphia now, within the reach of almost every man and woman who hears me speak to-night." Read that sentence again, but instead of "Philadelphia", replace it with your own market. Read it slowly and feel the weight of the truth in those words.

- Wealth and honesty are two separate things. Do not confuse the two. Always set a high ethical standard and pursue wealth – and enjoy the freedom your wealth brings.

- Wealth allows us to help others – such as by providing them with jobs, or by supporting charities that help those who cannot help themselves.

- Money is a tool; it's innate. It is used for good or evil purposes. So if you are consciously or unconsciously avoiding money because you've come to believe that it's bad, that makes as little sense as avoiding a screwdriver or pliers because you think they are bad.

- Our limiting beliefs entered our minds from as far back as our childhood – when our parents or teachers taught us something they believed, or demonstrated with their lives a belief they held. But just because they taught it or believed it, doesn't make it true. Your challenge is to identify that limiting belief about money and address it.

- Our beliefs about what we think we know shape how we act in the future. Will the things you know right now serve you in the future? Or do you need to change what you know?

- "There is wealth right within the sound of your voice" – that is a powerful statement and I urge you to embed it into your brain.

- What are people asking you for that you have been saying "no" to? Is there a skillset that is an untapped profit center for you?

- The more you understand your market, the greater the opportunities you'll find in that market. Before you stretch yourself too thin in multiple markets, ask yourself whether you've fully "mined" the market you're currently in.

- Your family and your employees will benefit from your success. But make sure you don't just reward them; you should also train them in the skills that made you successful.

- In your market, what do people need? What's in demand? What are the big problems to be solved? Answer that question (and keep asking and answering it regularly) and you have the key to limitless wealth.

- In your business, you might be tempted by "greener pastures" (whether that is a market to serve, or the employees you're trying hire, or some other thing you assume is better elsewhere). Remember that opportunity exists everywhere for those Warriors who step up!

- Lack of capital is a huge limiting belief. What other limiting beliefs are holding you back? As you read the story in *Acres Of Diamonds*, consider how it applies to your life – perhaps you think capital (or some other thing) is holding you back.

- Not sure how to invest in your business to grow? It's simple – find out what your customers want and need, and figure out how you can deliver it.

- There is money right under your chin if you would only look!

- Do you think of yourself as an innovator in your industry? Most wouldn't dare think of themselves that way but what would be possible if you did?

- History's greatest people achieved their success, fame, and historical permanence because they stepped up when it was required of them. If you are reading this, it's required of you as well! Your family and your employees need you to be great. Step up!

- "Whatsoever he had to do at all, he put his whole mind into it and held it all there until that was all done." Make that your daily practice at every task and you will be amazed at the results!

- You make your own reality. If you get caught up in the problems and challenges in your business, that negative viewpoint will come to define your business (which will, in turn, impact your attitude, your productivity, your hiring practices, your sales, your service, and even your health). Remember this: you make your own reality. Talk down your challenges and talk up your accomplishments and opportunities.

- Actions, not words, are the purest form of greatness. If you want to be great, ACT great in all aspects of your life and business.

- Your team doesn't need you to be the smartest or best speaker – you just need to lead them with power.

- You once worked on the front lines of your industry and you might be struggling to make the adjustment to lead your team. But if you want to own a service business, it's time to change your mindset. Your team needs you directing them from a higher vantage point.

- Warriors step up to the challenge and privilege of greatness. If you want to be successful in your business, it's time for to step up to greatness.

Warrior Wisdom From *The Art Of Money-Getting*

- There are unlimited opportunities to make money.

- Don't focus on the little things when you should be spending more time on the big things.

- This is a major problem today – people are spending more money than they make. How are you handling your money?

- "It requires some training, perhaps, to accomplish this economy, but when once used to it, you will find there is more satisfaction in rational saving than in irrational spending." I'm not advocating that you be stingy. Rather, I'm urging you to know what your income is and what your expenses are and to keep them both under firm control.

- What can be measured is managed. Track everything if you want to know the truth about anything.

- Many of our decisions are built around how we want to be perceived. When you stop caring what others think of you, you'll achieve a level of freedom to pursue what really matters in life.

- Wealth and freedom are possible but only if you gain mastery over the things that threaten wealth and freedom.

- What are your "guilty pleasures" that are costing you wealth and freedom?

- How is your health? What aspect of your health have you not yet mastered? (Hint: it could be holding you back from wealth and freedom.)

- What habits were once idle pleasures that have now become your master? (I'm speaking of addictions here – even to seemingly innocent addictions like coffee, social media, or the praise of others.) It's very hard to spot these in your life but they are holding you back from achieving greatness.

- Health is a foundational requirement for wealth and freedom. If you want wealth and freedom, you MUST get healthy.

- Take an inventory of your skills, then leverage those strengths and hire others to shore up your weaknesses.

- Businesses owners must seek out opportunities rather than operating their business wherever habit or traditional tell them.

- Shift your business to be where the opportunities are instead of wondering why there are no opportunities where your business is right now.

- Treat your debt as a tool (just as you'd treat money). Only use debt when you can build something with it.

- Your inner drive creates a business, your business creates wealth, and your wealth creates freedom. Invest in your drive, your business, and your wealth. When done correctly, these will grow even when you're not actively working in them.

- Set targets and NEVER stop pushing toward those targets.

- Perseverance is one of two ingredients necessary for success. (The other is hard work.)

- Hard work is one of two ingredients necessary for success. (The other is perseverance.)

- In every experience we win – we either achieve victory or we learn in defeat.

- There is no such thing as luck. Chance may occasionally influence our situation but we direct our paths. Your success is entirely dependent on you.

- A great team is one of the best investments you can make in your business. Pay more for the great ones, and hire too many – and your business will grow.

- "Go on in confidence, study the rules, and above all things, study human nature." This is a powerful strategy of growth in your business. Apply it!

- The home service industry is a noble trade to be in. Be proud of your contribution to making people's lives better, and do what you can to attract the next generation to the industry.

- Plan; work the plan relentlessly; measure; adjust your course but stay focused; persevere until success. Repeat.

- A Warrior understands and uses the power of focus, while others stand back in awe of how much the Warrior achieves.

- Within systems and routine, there is great freedom. This seems counter-intuitive to those who are not in a routine but once you create a system and start it, you'll discover more freedom than you ever thought possible.

- Don't get caught up in the negative headlines, but remain aware of the events and trends in the world and in your market and seek to understand how you can benefit from them.

- Maximize your marketing effectiveness by increasing the frequency of your marketing exposure.

- In today's world, we need to be MORE than polite and kind to customers – we need to WOW them with amazing service.

- Think carefully about how you define success. What does success mean to you? This definition will guide all decision-making.

Warrior Wisdom From *An Iron Will*

- The mastery of your will is everything. All success and failure hinges on whether or not you can master your will.

- Warriors willingly do what others will not. As a result, they'll reap the rewards that others will not.

- Your ability to concentrate on the task at hand will erase any barrier to productivity.

- Challenge yourself daily to increasing your willpower. There is no better exercise of your mind.

- Your willpower IS your power. Want more power? Get more willpower.

- There is strength in deciding and then acting with 100% conviction on that decision.

- A successful person is a master of willpower. An unsuccessful person is mastered by outside forces.

- There are three kinds of people in the world – the wills, the won'ts, and the can'ts. Which one are you? Which ones are on your team? Which ones are you hiring? Which ones are you training?

- It is willpower and NOT ability or intelligence or capital or even the right team that will determine your business success.

- The proof of willpower is in the results. If you are struggling in your results, you lack willpower.

- Willpower is conscious thought. Like a light that emits from your mind, your willpower could be faint glimmer or it can be a laser beam with the strength to cut steel.

- Willpower starts with a strong belief in yourself and what you can offer the world.

- Replenish your willpower by reviewing your foundational "why".

- Think something is impossible? Apply willpower.

- Willpower starts as a decision and continues as tireless persistence.

- Master your health and you'll build a foundation on which to create success.

- Personal discipline is a cornerstone of willpower. You cannot follow the whims of your desires and be a master of yourself.

- When faced with setbacks, your willpower will get you through. How much willpower are you building in your life?

- You decide everything – your health, your wealth, your level of success, your happiness, and more. It all starts in your mind.

- "Our antagonist is our helper." Those battles you fight and hardships you endure make your willpower stronger. The true Warrior with the strongest willpower seeks out hardships.

- In what aspects of your business do you lack nerve?

- Are you defined by your difficulties? That's a good thing… Only if they become the starting point for a new story of success that is fueled by willpower.

- The first step to succeeding with willpower is to take the first step.

- A Warrior's success is forged in the furnace of difficulty.

- What do you do when faced with impossibility?

- What is your purpose? What keeps you going when others around you give up?

- "Success is not measured by what a man accomplishes, but by the opposition he has encountered, and the courage with which he has maintained the struggle against overwhelming odds." Read that again and again until it is real in your life.

Warrior Wisdom From *As A Man Thinketh*

- "Man is made or unmade by himself; in the armoury of thought he forges the weapons by which he destroys himself; he also fashions the tools with which he builds for himself heavenly mansions of joy and strength and peace." Your thoughts become your reality. Are your negative thoughts destroying you or your positive thoughts building you up?

- You are the master of your thoughts.

- "As a being of Power, Intelligence, and Love, and the lord of his own thoughts, man holds the key to every situation, and contains within himself that transforming and regenerative agency by which he may make himself what he wills." Read that paragraph again! In your thoughts, you hold the key to every situation!

- Your life is a reflection of your thoughts. If you are not happy with your life, change how you think.

- Every thought becomes your reality in some way. So, what thoughts are you thinking? (That answer will predict your reality in the upcoming weeks, months, and years.)

- If you are frustrated or upset or annoyed about something, it's because there is misalignment between what you think should be happening and what is actually happening. The negativity will vanish when you achieve alignment.

- Improve your thoughts to improve your life. One must always come before the other.

- What is true for yourself is also true for your team and your family. If there is negativity, anger, frustration, or bad behavior, it's because there's misalignment between inner thoughts and outer circumstances. You can serve these people by helping them find alignment.

- Since thoughts become our reality, you can master your reality by mastering your thoughts.

- Indulgence and a lack of self-discipline will corrupt our thought processes and negatively alter our reality.

- Thoughts become reality, even in our body. Are you thinking about your health?

- A key indicator of thought-mastery is a clearly defined purpose. What's your purpose?

- Thought-mastery is not something you leave up to chance. You need to practice thought mastery.

- Are you a slave to your thoughts? If you have bad habits or addictions, or if you struggle with acquiring good habits, then you are a slave to your thoughts.

- The recipe for success is simple: master your thoughts, direct them toward a target, then take massive relentless action.

- Since our thoughts become our reality, start thinking big, powerful thoughts!

- A Warrior is always ready for battle but always surprisingly calm.

CONCLUSION

You have started on a journey. You started the day you were born but sometimes the events and circumstances of life pull you off track. You advanced your journey when you started your service business but sometimes the events and circumstances that you face every day continue to pull you off track.

Your destination? It's the level of success, freedom, and the personal and professional achievement that you aspire to have, as well as the legacy you hope to leave behind.

How will you look back and remember the life you lived? What will you leave behind? What will people remember you for?

Some people on life's journey might aspire to great things but they are convinced by society to live comfortable, secure, convenient lives where they barely rise to the occasion and would rather spend their downtime in front of the television. But if you build a powerful vision of what you want to achieve, and if you reach deep inside of you and tap into the Warrior that lies dormant within you, then you can push your way to a greater level of success and wealth, a higher level of personal and professional achievement, and a more meaningful legacy than you could ever possibly imagine – and you can do it sooner than you thought possible – only by becoming a Warrior.

My journey in life is to help other people become Warriors – in their service businesses and in their lives. That's why I founded CEO Warrior. That's why I work one-on-one with the Warriors in my exclusive Warrior Circle. That's why I hold 4-day Warrior Fast Track Academy events.

And that's also why I sent you this book. I want to help you on your journey toward whatever you aspire to be, to do, and to have, and I want help you access the Warrior within you. This book is, in my opinion, essential reading on your journey. It's a book that shares the wisdom and thinking of Warrior-like thought-leaders who pioneered the ideas and strategies that you can apply on your journey.

In this book you read Russell Conwell's *Acres Of Diamonds* as he shared how the opportunities of life are right in front of you if you will only see them and grasp them, and he explained what it takes to become great in whatever you set your mind to. It's easy to get caught up looking elsewhere but there are untapped opportunities in your life and business right now!

You also read P. T. Barnum's *The Art Of Money-Getting*, as this famous business owner shared strategy after strategy to help you start, run, and grow a business based on the foundational principles that haven't changed since he wrote them. Barnum tells us that there is an almost unlimited opportunity to make money as long as we watch our income and expenses, treat customers well, and advertise.

You read Orison Swett Marden's *An Iron Will*, which is a profound and passionate explanation of the one thing that separates successful people from unsuccessful ones: willpower. Want a simple test to see how well you understood and applied Marden's writing? Try breaking your worst habit and see if you were able to overcome the temptation to return to that habit. If not, go back and read Marden's book again. If success has eluded you (whether that's success in business, wealth, relationships, or anything else), you need to master your willpower and Marden's book will guide you.

And, you read James Allen's *As A Man Thinketh*, which explains that your thoughts become your reality. So the question is: what are you thinking about? That will very shortly become reality for you. Most people think little thoughts and create little realities but if you're a Warrior, you'll start thinking big thoughts and create big realities.

I hope you have pages upon pages of notes from these four writers. Some of the notes will be directly connected to your life and business, and will be actionable right away. Many of your notes might just be interesting to think about for now but you'll continue to gain a ton of clarity and insight and alignment from these notes whenever you read this book. (I encourage you to read it at least once a year).

Are you living the life you want? If you answered "yes" then that's great news... And you can expand that amazing life with the tools, strategies, and wisdom contained in these pages. But if you answered "no" (and many people do answer that way when they're honest with themselves) then **this book can be a guide for you to transform your life to become whatever it is you want it to be. It's all here. Now it's time to use it.**

Now that you've reached the end of the book, here's what you should do next...

1. **Read this book again**: always actively read the book with highlighter, pen, paper, and sticky notes nearby. Every time you read this book, no matter what level your business is at, actively reading it will help you derive more solid action steps that you can implement. Schedule time

to read the book from front to back annually, and schedule time each week to refer to a chapter and take action on that chapter. That way, you're always working **on** your business (not **in** your business) using this book as a guide.

2. **Complete the action steps**: this book is not just a document of information; it's a document of transformative action. Throughout this book you've made lists of action steps. Now I want you to perform those action steps in your life and business. Take action always! (And when you read the book again, you'll create more action steps that you should implement right away.)

3. **Bookmark CEOWARRIOR.com**: you'll find a wealth of resources to help you, including a blog, and videos. Become familiar with this website and refer to it often.

4. **Sign up for weekly money making tips**: this is a must-read newsletter that arrives in your email inbox weekly. Sign up for it at CEOWARRIOR.com and watch your inbox for each issue.

5. **Connect with me on social media:** Visit CEOWARRIOR.com to find all the social media channels we can connect on.

Welcome to the journey toward becoming a Warrior and achieving everything you want in business and in life. Welcome to a whole new world where you discover the Warrior within you that has been dormant for so long. We're only just scratching the surface of what your life could be. I am honored to share the life-transforming strategies in this book with you, I look forward to watching you grow in your life, and I hope to add even more massive value to your life as you continue your journey to become a **Warrior**.

GET ON THE FAST TRACK BY CREATING POWERFUL CHANGE IN YOUR BUSINESS

You've learned a lot in this book. Now it's time to implement it. On the following pages, you'll find powerful game-changing ways that can help you take what you've learned in this book and implement it into your business.

You'll connect directly with Mike and learn from him as he walks you through these areas of mastery. You'll create a powerful blueprint for your business (and your life). You'll be amazed at the changes.

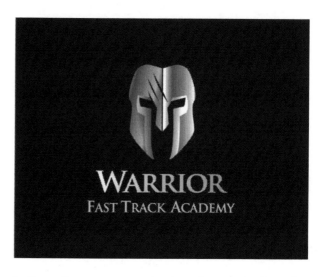

Are you tired of treading water – staying busy in your business but never really getting ahead? Are you ready to discover the most powerful strategies to create real change, growth, and market domination in your business?

Whether you're new and totally overwhelmed or you're a seasoned pro and looking for to reignite, the Warrior Fast Track Academy can show you how to get to the next level.

Warrior Fast Track Academy is my 4-day hands-on event where I guide you and a group of like-minded service business owners through the exact plan that I used to build a $28 million (and growing) business. I'll reveal the blueprint and show you how you can implement the same blueprint into **your** business, with all areas of mastery planned out and ready to be plugged in. You'll be motivated and inspired to lead positive, profitable change in your company and take your business to never-before-seen heights.

Business owners who have attended the Warrior Fast Track Academy have said it's "life changing" and have gone on to build successful multi-million dollar businesses all around the world.

If you want to take control of your business and your future, Warrior Fast Track Academy is THE event to make that happen. To see what others are saying about Warrior Fast Track Academy, and to pre-register for an upcoming event, go to WarriorFastTrackAcademy.com.

Have you ever wished you had a "Warrior Family" that could simultaneously hold you accountable for growing beyond your best self – and at the same time support your quest to get there?

Congratulations, you're home! If you elect to join the CEO Warrior Circle, this is what we do.

During the upcoming year, we will revolutionize your business and your life together. The CEO Warrior Circle is committed to simplicity and balance. Together, we'll blow your wealth, freedom and personal goals out of the water by focusing on massive business-building and life-transforming strategies.

We will also support you as you incorporate the 5 Dimensions of Life and Business Mastery – **Belief, Relationships, Health, Wealth, and Freedom** – and help you design activities and surroundings to support an amazing life!

This program is designed for go-getters and people who are ready to make the commitment and take action to boost their business.

To learn more about the Warrior Circle, and to see if you qualify to participate in the Mastermind, get in touch at <u>CEOWARRIOR.com/contact</u>.

Read Mike's Other Books

Mike Agugliaro is the author of a growing list of books and programs written for service business owners and entrepreneurs who want massive transformation and growth in their lives and businesses, and who want wealth, freedom, and market domination.

His first book, *The Secrets Of Business Mastery* is a popular book that explains how service business owners can achieve mastery and success in 12 areas. This is not just a business book but a powerful book of strategies to take charge of your life, too. You'll learn how to master yourself, your time, your finances, your team, your systems, your future, and so much more.

This 200+ page book is packed with valuable and highly actionable strategies.

If you want more purpose-specific guidance then you should read his shorter, practical, hands-on guides:
- *Secrets Of Leadership Mastery*
- *Secrets Of Communication Mastery*

These books will transform how you interact with others. They should be mandatory reading for anyone in your business who leads a team or communicates with other team members, vendors, or customers.

Mike is also the creator of *The Nine Pillars Of Business Mastery*, a powerful 9-step system that will help you instantly master any skill or strategy, or overcome any problem or habit. It's the result of years of study and testing and it's the source of massive change for anyone who reads and applies it.

See all of Mike's books at CEOWARRIOR.com/books.

Read The Free Magazine Written For The Home Service Industry

Discover new information, insight, and industry-specific success stories in **Home ServiceMAX** – the free online magazine written for home service business owners.

Each issue of Home ServiceMAX is packed with practical tips and strategies that you can implement right away into your home service business. They're field-tested and written by experts and industry insiders.

Home ServiceMAX will help you improve your sales, marketing, finance, human resources and customer service. Keep it on hand as you develop best practices to meet your team's unique challenges.

Whether you're a plumber, electrician, carpenter, roofer, builder, painter or specialist in any other service industry trade, to survive you must also stand out as a business leader. We designed this magazine to help you achieve that goal.

Each easy-to-read issue is available online for free. Check out the articles and make sure you have a pen and paper in hand to write down all the actions you'll want to take when you're done each article.

Read the current issue and subscribe here: **HomeServiceMaxMag.com**.

ABOUT THE AUTHOR

 As Seen On

Mike Agugliaro helps his clients grow their service businesses utilizing his $28 Million Warrior Fast Track Academy Blueprint, which teaches them how to achieve massive wealth and market domination.

Two decades ago, he founded Gold Medal Electric with his business partner Rob. After nearly burning out, he and Rob made a change: they developed a powerful blueprint that grew the company. Today, Gold Medal

Service is now the top service industry provider in Central New Jersey. With over 180 staff and 120 trucks on the road, Gold Medal Service now earns over $28 million in revenue each year.

Mike is a transformer who helps service business owners and other entrepreneurs master themselves and their businesses, take control of their dreams and choices, and accelerate their life and business growth to new heights. Mike is the author of the popular book *The Secrets Of Business Mastery*, in which he reveals 12 areas that all service business owners need to master, as well as other books like *Secrets Of Leadership Mastery*, and *Secrets Of Communication Mastery*. And, his *9 Pillars of Business Mastery* is an online resource that is changing the lives of aspiring Warriors around the world.

Mike speaks and transforms around the world; his Warrior Fast Track Academy events are popular, transformational events for service business owners; he also leads a mastermind of business owners known as Warrior Circle. Mike has been featured in MSNBC, Financial Times, MoneyShow, CEO World, and more.

Mike is an avid martial artist who has studied karate, weaponry, jujitsu, and has even developed his own martial art and teaches it to others. The discipline of martial arts equips him to see and act on opportunities, create change in himself and others, and see that change through to successful completion.

Mike is a licensed electrician and electrical inspector, he is a certified Master Fire Walk Instructor, certified professional speaker, and a licensed practitioner of Neuro-Linguistic Programming (NLP).

Whether firewalking, breaking arrows on his neck, studying martial arts, transforming businesses, or running his own business, Mike Agugliaro leads by powerful example and is changing the lives and businesses of service business owners everywhere.

Mike lives in New Jersey with his wife and two children.

CONNECT WITH MIKE AGUGLIARO

Connect with me in the following places:

Website: **CEOWARRIOR.com**

Podcast: **CEOWARRIOR.com/podcast**

Events: **WarriorFastTrackAcademy.com**

Social: Visit **CEOWARRIOR.com** to connect with Mike on Facebook, Twitter, LinkedIn, Instagram, and elsewhere.

Home ServiceMAX Magazine: **HomeServiceMaxMag.com**

Made in the USA
Middletown, DE
19 April 2016